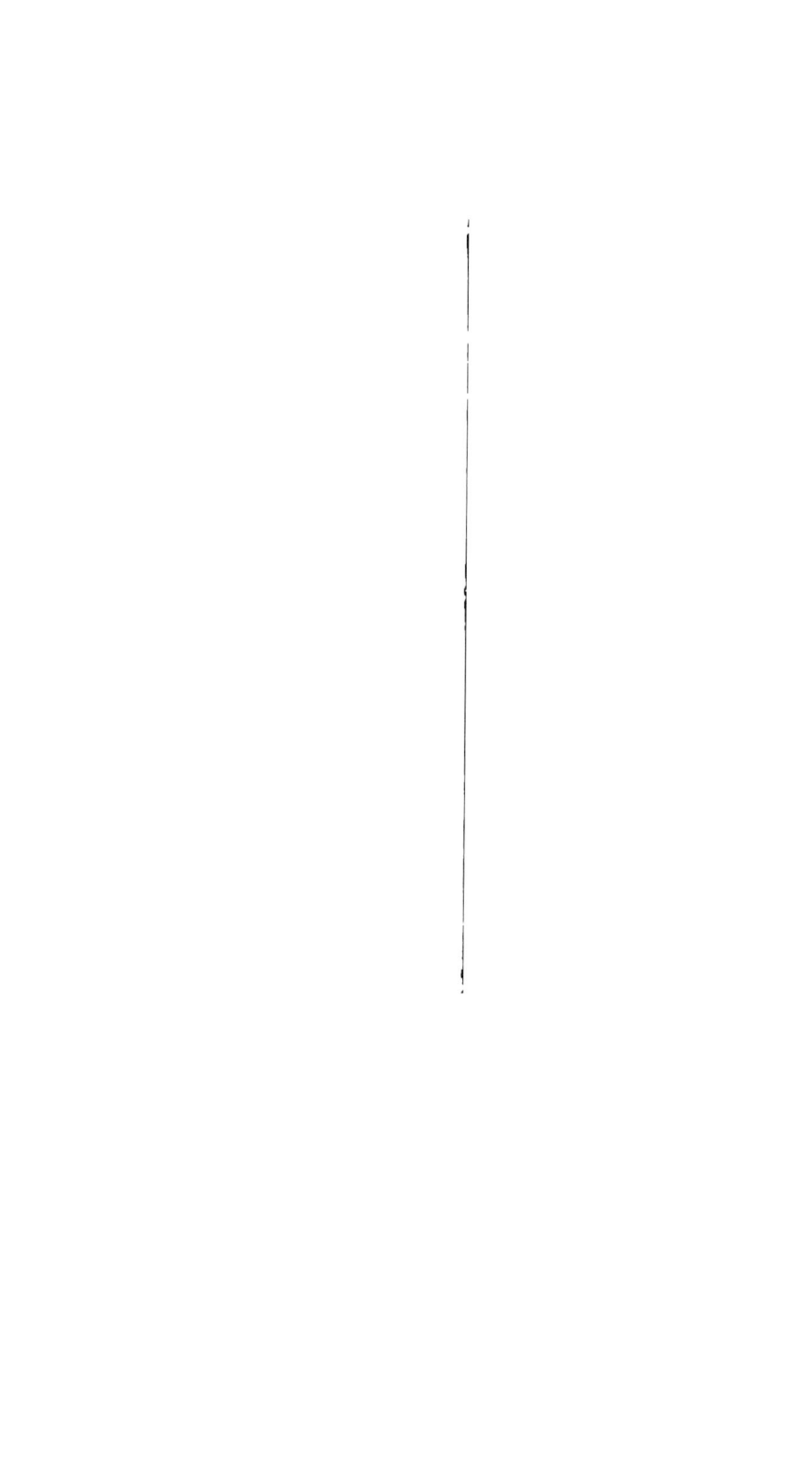

DERBY,
from the East.

THE HISTORY OF DERBY;

FROM THE REMOTE AGES OF ANTIQUITY
TO THE YEAR MDCCXCI.

DESCRIBING

ITS SITUATION, AIR, SOIL, WATER, STREETS,
BUILDINGS, AND GOVERNMENT.

WITH THE ILLUSTRIOUS FAMILIES WHICH HAVE
INHERITED ITS HONOURS.

ALSO ITS

Ecclesiastical History,

TRADE, AMUSEMENTS, REMARKABLE OCCURRENCES,
AND EMINENT MEN;

WITH THE ADJACENT SEATS OF THE GENTRY.

ILLUSTRATED WITH XIX. PLATES.

By W. HUTTON, F. A. S. S.

THE SECOND EDITION, WITH ADDITIONS.

LONDON:
PRINTED BY AND FOR NICHOLS, SON, AND BENTLEY,
Red Lion Passage, Fleet Street.
SOLD ALSO BY BALDWIN, CRADOCK, AND JOY,
PATERNOSTER-ROW; AND BY ALL THE BOOKSELLERS IN
DERBY, BIRMINGHAM, LEICESTER, AND NOTTINGHAM.
1817.

HARVARD COLLEGE
JUN 24 1927
LIBRARY
Hayes fund

ADVERTISEMENT.

THE public attention having been particularly directed to the various publications of Mr. HUTTON, by the interesting "Life" of himself, recently published by his Daughter, I have been induced to re-print a small impression of his "History of Derby." From the pleasing and unaffected style in which the Work is written, it cannot fail, I trust, to be equally well received with the first Edition, which has been a long time out of print, and very scarce.

I have availed myself of the later publication of the Rev. D. P. Davies's "History of Derbyshire," to make a few additions.

Nov. 1, 1817. J. B. NICHOLS.

PLATES.

Prospect of Derby . . . . *to face the Title page.*
Plan of the Town . . . . Page 19
St. Mary's Bridge 30
County Hall 32
Guildhall 33
Free School 35
Prison 37
Devonshire Alms Houses 42
Black Alms Houses 43
Widows Alms Houses 44
Assembly 48
Theatre 50
St. Alkmund's Church 115
St. Michael's 118
St. Warburgh's 119
St. Peter's 121
All Saints 123
Meeting in Friar-gate 139
Independent Meeting House 141

TO

FRANCIS ASHBY, Esq.

MAYOR OF DERBY, 1791.

SIR,

IT is not from personal acquaintance that I address you, for I never had the pleasure of seeing you; nor from the hope of a lucrative return; I neither wish nor want any: but because you are the Chief Magistrate of an antient Borough, which gave birth to those affections which it now possesses. When I departed from the place, it did not depart from my esteem. Whenever I gain a sight of those turrets, over which you preside, it diffuses a sensation through the mind, like the discovery of an

old

old acquaintance, in whose favour I have been long and warmly interested. If asked, Why, in this address, I do not comprehend the whole Corporate Body? I answer, I cannot take the head without including the members.

PREFACE.

A BODY of history, like that of a man, is composed of minute parts, every one of which ought to be known; otherwise the whole will be defective. No topographical history can be complete till its detached parts are investigated; and this task is the most likely to be correct when performed by a resident. Every piece of local history, like a mite cast into the treasury, tends to furnish the sum wanted.

Two requisites form an Historian: to convey all which ought to be conveyed; and that in a pleasing manner. How far I have succeeded in both, must be left to the Reader. The first consists in the assiduity in collecting materials; in this I
have

have not been defective; also, in selecting them with judgement: and the second is more the gift of nature than the acquirement of art.

I took up the pen at that period in which most writers lay it down. I may be said to have set off upon my historical pursuits from the vale of years, at a time when every declining year, like every minute of a declining sun, tells five.

The only ancient authors who have spoken materially of Derby, are Leland and Camden. Both are short; nor is it a wonder that he who grasps at much, loses nearly all. No one ever wrote a history of the place, although it has long merited one. I therefore tread that ground, where was first cast my severe lot; where, at an early age, I was attacked with most of the ills attendant upon human life, without the power either of resistance or retreat.

I am indebted to Richard Gough, Esq. for his valuable edition of the Britannia.

I have

I have also to express my obligations to the Rev. Mr. Manlove, Mr. Alderman Eaton, and Mr. Swift, for the information I received; but still more for the politeness with which I was received myself. A favour communicated with civility doubles its value.

Another debt I contracted with the Reverend James Pilkington, who recently published " The Present State of Derbyshire," and this in a manner perfectly new. He professes not to follow the dry Dugdale; and his work verifies the assertion: to read Dugdale is a drudgery; but to peruse Pilkington, a delight. One conveys intelligence without pleasure ; the other conveys both. Our performances, though in a small degree upon the same subject, widely differ; but, I trust, not in every respect. I have made free with many passages in his valuable work, without directing the Reader to the source whence I drew them, that I might not break the line of his attention, by removing his eye to the margin. And I embrace
this

this public mode of conveying my gratitude for the information he has given, and the trouble he has saved me. Had not he examined dusty charters and mouldy records, I must. A part of my knowledge is grafted upon his assiduity. Had his production seen the light a little sooner, mine would for ever have been hid. But when I first heard of *his*, this work was too far advanced, for the pride of an Author, to be given up to destruction.

Unknown in Derby, I stand clear of prejudice. When I silently wander from the extremity of St. Mary's Bridge to that of St. Peter's parish, without meeting one face that I know, I consider myself a stranger at home; but though forgotten, I cannot forget. I behold with concern the buildings altered with time; and reflect, with a sigh, that every house has changed its inhabitants; and that I have to mourn a whole generation, who are swept into the grave.

CONTENTS.

	Page
Name	1
Situation	6
Public Roads	8
Soil	9
Air	10
Water	ib.
Antiquity	12
The Castle	17
The Streets	19
Publick Buildings	26
County Hall, or Court of Justice	32
Guildhall	33
Free School	35
Prisons	37
Alms Houses	41
Infirmary	46
Ordnance Depot	47
Assembly	48
Theatre	50
Workhouses	ib.
Earls of Derby	54
Government	68
A List of the Bailiffs and Mayors	78
Members for the Borough	91
Fairs	103

Court

xii   CONTENTS.

	Page.
Court of Requests	104
Ecclesiastical History	105
Churches	115
St. Alkmund's	ib.
St. Michael's	118
St. Warburgh's	119
St. Peter's	121
All Saints	123
Dissenters	139
Meeting in Friar-gate	ib.
Methodists	140
Independents	141
Religious Houses	ib.
St. Helen's	142
St. Mary de Pratis	145
Dominican Friars	147
St. James's	148
Maison de Dieu and St. Leonard	150
St. Mary's	151
Trade	154
Silk-mill	158
Navigation	172
Mills	173
Porcelain	ib.
Jewellery	177
Spar	178
Cotton	180
Amusements	181
Occurrences	185
Eminent Men	228
Gentlemen's Seats near Derby	250

THE HISTORY
OF
DERBY.

NAME.

No man treads upon ground so uncertain as the Antiquary. When he has collected all the lights he is able, he is sometimes doubtful of his way. Traditions, arguments, evidences, by turns explain and bewilder. Other pursuits are clear; his are dubious. Contradictions offer, which he cannot reconcile. *Right* and *wrong* are his inseparable companions; he can discharge neither; let him then discriminate both.

We are informed, by our Historians, that the name of this place, during the Heptarchy,

Heptarchy, was *Northworthig;* but no reason is offered to support it, nor any explanation given. If the distance of time has denied proof, we might, at least, expect an argument. If this was the Saxon name, we should naturally enquire, which then was *Southworthig?* for it must have had an opposite. — Tamworth is produced as the counter name, *Tamworthage?* but the names unfortunately are as wide as the places. Supposing, however, this was the Saxon name, it must have had another, both under the Romans and the Britons: it is our province to seek it.

There are two sources from whence the name of *Derby* may have been drawn, one antecedent, the other subsequent, to the Saxons; but as only one can be the *true*, I shall describe both, give my sentiments, and not quarrel with the Reader for his.

We are told by tradition, which very often tells truth, that *Little Chester*, half a mile above Derby, upon the Derwent, was a Roman city; and that Derby was a gentleman's park, stocked with deer; hence the

the name *Deer-by*. This is corroborated by the town arms, a Buck couchant in a Park. An able antagonist might support this hypothesis against another who supported a better; they might sustain the contest as long as the siege of Troy, both claim the victory, and sing *Te Deum*, but neither win it. That Little Chester was a Roman station is certain; the name, the coins, the fort, the bridge, and particularly the Ikenield street, confirm it. Though denominated a *City*, it was but small; this is proved by the foundations, which are not extensive.

But there are many reasons why the name of *Derby* could not be derived as above. A Park was not known in England till the arrival of the Normans, nor Coat Armoury till a much later period. Arms were first granted to the military hero as a badge of honour; and his successor, though degenerate, took care to retain it. If the Patriarchs are charged with emblematical devices representative of character; if the Romans brought an Eagle, the

Saxons a White Horse, and the Danes a Raven; yet they were only ensigns to distinguish their several countries, which had no connexion with Heraldry; and although coats of arms are ascribed to some of our Saxon Kings, they were given by the Heralds of modern date. Not an instance can be produced of a coat of arms till about the tenth century. Nor did they prevail as a fashion till those diabolical adventures, which disgrace the Christian name, *the Crusades,* when the innocent inhabitants of Palestine were butchered because they possessed the Land of Miracles. It follows that those coats of arms with crosses claim a pre-eminence in antiquity. As Derby was a town of considerable magnitude many centuries prior to either the Park or the Arms, it could not derive its name from *Deer in a park;* a modern is not likely to confer one upon an ancient; we must therefore penetrate further back for a solution. The name of the town, and of the river *Derwent* upon which it stands, have the same origin; the word is of British extraction,

extraction, and means *to move swift*, which answers to the motion of the stream. Hence it follows, that the river, being something older than the town, gave it the name *Derwentby*, or the town by the Derwent; afterwards corrupted into *Deroby*, now *Derby*. Even this Roman city itself derived its name *Derventio* from the same river. *Derley* also, the next village upon the opposite bank, will decide the contest; its name is derived from the same source, *Der* from the river, and *ley*, which is British, signifying a home. Ten or fifteen miles up the stream, is another *Derley* of exactly the same derivation. The *Buck in the park* probably arose from the whim of some ignorant magistrate, and has no more affinity with the place than the *coronet and ragged staff has with Nottingham*. A person of the name of *Slater* assured me, that his family resided at the foot of the bridge three hundred years ago, while the site of Derby was a park. One of his wise ancestors probably was Bailiff when the arms were obtained.

SITUATION.

SITUATION.

Derby lies in an open valley, low, but not flat. Most of the town is situated upon a peninsula formed by the junction of two rivers, the Derwent and Markeaton brook. Friar-gate, Wardwick, Peter-gate, Baglane, and part of Morlege, are nearly all the parts which extend beyond. If we draw a line from St. Mary's bridge to the brook upon Nuns-green, we shall find it perhaps half a mile. Another line from the centre of this to Tennant bridge, the distance will be found about the same. Hence the peninsula becomes a triangle.

From each river the land rises to the centre, perhaps sixteen feet, which forms a summit, or ridge, upon which stand three churches in a line, All Saints, St. Michael's, and St. Alkmund's. The remainder of the town beyond the brook, upon which stands St. Peter's, rises about the same height.

The manor is bounded on the North by Chester, Derley, and Allestry; on the
West

West by Markeaton; on the South by Great and Little Over, Normanton, and Osmaston; and on the East by Bolton, Alvaston, and Chaddesdon. The lordship is nearly circular, is two miles in diameter, and contains more than two thousand acres. The town stands, and the Derwent runs, nearly in the centre. There is no waste land, except Nuns-green, which in my time was rough as a brick-yard, but now improved into pleasure ground. The Corporation are lords of the manor.

Most of the East side of the town is common lands for the use of the burgesses, as Bradshaw Hays, the Siddalls, the Holmes, the old Meadows, the Checker Closes, Cowsley Field, and the New Pasture. The burgesses loudly complain of their magistrates, for having pillaged their property, and appropriated it to their private use; but I should hope, for the honour of my native country, that no man would steal, except when he cannot be detected.

There are nine hamlets belonging to Derby, but they are only under ecclesiastical jurisdiction: Little-Chester, Derley, Little-Eaton, Quarndon, Normanton, Bolton, Litchurch, Alvaston, and Osmaston.

PUBLIC ROADS.

No circumstance respecting a town is of more consequence than the roads that surround it. This is the capital trait which marks the degree of improvement at which a people are arrived.

Eight roads proceed from Derby to the adjacent places, all turnpike:

To Nottingham	16 Miles.
Mansfield,	22
Worksworth,	13
Ashborn,	13
Uttoxeter,	19
Burton,	11
Ashby-de-la-Zouch,	14
Loughborough,	17

These are excellent, and are used with pleasure. But I knew them when the best
was

was incommodious even in summer, and scarcely passable in the winter. The bemired traveller found them as Nature left them; but now Art has improved upon Nature for his benefit. It is not possible to open a navigable river, or complete a public road, but the places to which they point must improve.

Derby has experienced the utility of both, which has brought conveniences, riches, and increase. These roads, however, have one defect: their constructors, not being obliged to walk on foot, forgot those who were, by neglecting the causeway.

SOIL.

The land in the vicinity of Derby is excellent, is in high cultivation, and lets at advanced rents, yet is eagerly sought after. No rock is found in or near the place. After penetrating a great depth of rich soil, we come to a loose blackish gravel. Clay is plentiful, which produces bricks of a fine colour and texture.

AIR.

AIR.

Much of health and longevity depends upon the water and air we draw into the system. Stagnate moisture is hurtful; but this is prevented by the air passing through an open valley, some miles over, which, admitting a free passage, promotes exhalation, and purifies itself. Derby is not remarkable either for long or short life. Agues are rather prevalent; rheumatisms are not.

Before we arrive at the last page of this short work, mention will often be made of that most dreadful of all diseases, which chiefly originates from stagnate filth, *The Plague.*

WATER

is never scarce, but is sometimes too plenttiful. Floods abound. The Derwent rises about twenty miles above Buxton, drains the Peak hills, and, tumbling over the little rocks, flows with rapidity. I have known

known these hills produce an inundation, without a drop of rain, at Derby.—Leland describes the Derwent as " rising plaine west, a little above Blackwell (*Bakewell*) a market-town, to Darle, in the Peke, to Wennesle village, and through Crumford bridge, to Wetstonde, Welbridge, to Darle, Darby, Sawle Feri (Sawley Ferry), five miles by land from Darby, where it goeth into Trente."

This river supplies the water for culinary use, which is raised by an engine at the bottom of St. Michael's lane, and conveyed through a pipe into a reservoir at the top of the church, about the distance of one hundred yards, and the height of twelve. From thence, as from a grand artery, the stream is conveyed by tubes, under the pavement, into almost every street and court. Perhaps this is the most useful church in Derby, though preached in but once a month.—Exclusive of this ample supply from the river, springs are common; the water, which is hard, lies within a few feet of the surface, and is raised by a pump.

Markeaton

Markeaton Brook, originally Hoddebrook, has its source a few miles off, and turns several mills before lost in the Derwent. I have known this little spirited brook, whose common depth does not exceed five inches, rise from its bed, about six feet below the ground floor, to within eighteen inches of the chamber; this happened in 1741, when the skies were set at liberty, after having been bound a whole year by the keen East, which had occasioned the hard frost.

There is another stream still less, yet able to turn a mill, which washes the banks of Derby, *Bramley Brook,* or rather *Bramble,* from its secret progress among the thorns. It rises a mile to the South, at the foot of Little-Over hills, and discharges itself into Markeaton brook, near the Wardwick.

ANTIQUITY.

Having examined the etymology of the name, the geography, boundaries, properties

ties, and appendages of the place, we must now extend our researches to those remote periods which afford neither light nor guide, where the benighted traveller is left to guess out his way by probability.

Under the British and Roman governments Derby was part of the territory of the *Coritani;* under the Saxon, the North of *Mercia;* and under the Norman, part of *Midland.*

All our Historians agree in charging Derby with great antiquity, but there are no memoirs, or monuments, to ascertain the date, neither does tradition throw any light upon its early existence. But there are many circumstantial evidences, which tend to prove it a place of some magnitude in the time of the Britons.—The situation is very inviting, upon a gentle ascent, in a flat, at the confluence of two valuable rivers, adapted for use and security, and exactly suited to the taste of our British ancestors.—A passage over the Derwent was absolutely necessary in very early ages to connect the Eastern and the Western banks.

St.

St. Mary's bridge, therefore, in various forms, must have been that passage, because there are not the least vestiges of another in that part of the country, nor any roads with which another *could* connect, that at Little Chester excepted, the history of which is well known.—It was a point with the Romans, in forming their famous military ways, to direct them *by* the British towns, but never *through* them. This was the case at Derby. The Ikenield-street, one of their grand roads, which I have described in another work, runs *by* Sutton-Coldfield, Lichfield, Burton, Derby, Chesterfield, &c. which is a further proof of its great antiquity. At regular distances they erected castles, or stations, guarded by the Roman soldiers, to preserve their dominion over the natives, and to prevent a connexion with them. At *Derventio* (Little-Chester) the Roman power is marked in visible characters. Over the Derwent, at this spot, they erected a bridge, not for the use of the Britons, but themselves; the foundations are yet seen in clear water; I have

have felt them with the oar. This ancient bridge indicates that one more antient must have been used at St. Mary's, perhaps many centuries prior to the Romans.

The five churches are another proof of its great antiquity. Derby never was larger than at present, yet is overstocked with churches; it follows, it could not have been much smaller, or there would have been no need of five. It is ridiculous to build churches without inhabitants to use them. As these are of Saxon origin, the town appears to have been nearly as large a thousand years ago as now. From its slow growth, therefore, it must have taken many ages to arrive at its Saxon magnitude. As the increase was never rapid *since* the reach of history, we may fairly conclude it never was before. I was present, in 1738, at a conversation between two natives, when one challenged the other to produce an instance in Derby of a house being built upon a *new foundation*. The affirmative, I well remember, was not proved; which shews that a very small, or
rather

rather *no* increase attended it. I allow, the river being open, the silk trade multiplied, the roads improved, the china-work established, &c. has given it an addition.

Again, it is certainly one of the most ancient boroughs in the kingdom, which is another reason in favour of its being one of the most ancient towns. As there never was any staple commerce, or any incident that could augment the number of inhabitants, they must have proceeded in still life for ages, without much increase or diminution.—Its early magnitude is further proved by Halfden's forces being quartered there during the winter of 874, which supposes it a town of size.—Its being constituted the metropolis of the county in the reign of Alfred, proves it also to have been, in that early age, a place of consideration; and its not being central is a further proof, because a place so situated, of equal size, would have had the preference.

The confined state of some of the principal streets, as Iron-gate, Sadler-gate, Market-head, is another proof of its antiquity. In that

that remote period when they were first laid out, commerce was at a low ebb; the street was little used, never by carriages. A small space was sufficient for daily purpose; the scale of life was narrow, compared to the present; as may that of the present compared to the future. Neither was the light obstructed as in our day, because the houses were low, none exceeding one story.

THE CASTLE

is the ultimate indication of Antiquity I shall mention. A castle, as well as a church, left to the ravages of time, will endure an equal number of centuries. The last remains of the castle at Derby are said to have expired about two hundred years past. If it fell by old age, we may fairly allow a thousand years for its existence, one hundred for its decay, and two since; which is a reasonable allowance; and it will bring us near the Roman government, when it became requisite to guard so considerable a town, which had no other fortifications,

fications, with a castle. It is possible, however, that it might fall by violence, and no time so likely as in the quarrel between the Roses. The Lords of Derby being of the House of Lancaster, when that House fell, the wrath of the House of York might discharge its vengeance upon this castle.

If a Reader should be so fond of Antiquity as to merit the epithet of *an old castle hunter;* if, like me, he has waded up to the neck in furze, to see the Ikenield street; treasured up the jaw of a monk because the ground had preserved it a few centuries; dined at the King's head, in Fenchurch-street, out of a shattered dish, in which Queen Elizabeth breakfasted upon pork and peas, the morning she exchanged a prison for a throne; or hugged a broken chamber-pot which she had used; if he has dived into the bowels of the earth to bring up a Roman coin not worth three-halfpence; or preserved the fragments of an earthen vessel, out of which his great grandfather ate milk-porridge; he will not be displeased when I inform him, that he

may

may find the vestiges of this castle in Mrs. Chambers's orchard, on the summit of the hill. One of the mounds, eighty yards long, runs parallel with the houses upon Cock-pit-hill, perhaps one hundred yards behind them; also parallel with those in St. Peter's parish, but twice the distance. This place of security then stood out of the town in an open field; no houses were near. It was guarded by the Derwent on one side, and on the other ran the London road. This, I apprehend, was the chief approach, because the passage afterwards bore the name of *Castle-street*. From thence also the fields towards the East, now Mr. Borrow's park, acquired the name of *Castle-fields*.

THE STREETS.

Derby is said to be a mile long; that is, from St. Mary's bridge to Cuckold's alley; but it must be a very short one. Neither is the passage straight, but curves with the river. Its breadth, from the top of Friar-gate,

gate, through Sadler-gate to the Derwent, is nearly half a mile. Could the town be thrown into a square, it would not cover one hundred acres. The market-place is not large, but very neat, useful, and elegant, and is the first ornament of the place. There are about eighteen streets, but not more than six of these are central, as Queen-street, St. Mary-gate, Sadler-gate, Iron-gate, Rotton-row, and Corn-market; the others verge upon the borders.

One would think there was some motive for the name of every street; and yet it would puzzle the Antiquary to find the original of Walker-lane, St. Mary-gate, Bold-lane, Sadler-gate, Iron-gate, Rotten-row, and Bag-lane; perhaps they are the offspring of a proprietor's name or trade, or of fancy. King and Queen streets were probably so called in honour of the Royal owners during the Heptarchy, for the place was then a Royal borough. The inhabitants were considerable favourers of the Saints, by preserving their names in the streets, as St. Helen, St. James, St. Michael, St. Mary,

and

and St. Peter, which constitute a tolerable kalendar. Bridge-gate took its rise from St. Mary's bridge; and *that* from St. Mary's chapel; Nuns-green from a nunnery, otherwise The Willows, because abounding with that tree, but prior to either King's-mead : this was an appropriation of Burton Abbey, to which three peppercorns were annually paid as an acknowledgment of ownership ; Friar-gate from a house of Black-friars; Wardwick from *ward*, a detached place, and *wick*, a home, from the British; Corn-market, carries its own interpretation. Peter's parish, from the church, anciently as above, Peter-gate, and more antiently Castle-gate, because leading to that fortress. *Morlege*, from *Moor*, low, *lodge*, a house, with which it perfectly agrees. Full-street, from being the habitation of fullers, lying convenient for that calling from its vicinity to the water.

At the bottom of this street, upon the banks of the Derwent, twenty yards from the river, now Mr. Upton's garden, I first drew the vital air, September 30, 1723.

There

There are also eight bye lanes, slenderly inhabited; St. Helen's-walk, St. Michael's-lane, Nanny Tag's, Silk-mill, Leather, Babington, Green, and Dason Lanes, which barely excite the notice of an Historian.

The number of houses in Derby are said to be 1637, and the inhabitants 8563 *.

Many of the private buildings† deserve notice, as the house of Mrs. Wilmot, late Ayre's, in Peter's parish; that of —— Forester, Esq. in a vile situation in Babington-Lane: Captain Barns's, at the Brookside. In the Wardwick, a narrow street

* Derby has rapidly increased within these thirty years in size and number of inhabitants. By the Population Return to Parliament, in 1811, it appears that the Borough of Derby contained 34 houses building; 142 houses uninhabited; 2,644 inhabited houses; and 2,924 families (95 of which families were employed in Agriculture; 2,382 in trade, &c.; and 447 not comprised in the two preceeding classes); consisting of 5,978 males, and 7,065 females: total 13,043. EDIT.

† The reader must bear in mind that this is a list of the Gentry resident at Derby in 1791. EDIT.

with

with a gloomy aspect, we are pleased with
those of Thomas Wilson, Esq. Francis
Fox, Esq. William Smith, Esq. Samuel
Fox, Esq. Mr. Lowe, Mrs. Rolleston, and
Walter Mather, Esq. In Friar-gate, which
is spacious, but ill laid out, are those of
Samuel and —--- Crompton, Esquires, Lady
Wilmot, Mrs. Pickford, Mr. Lowe, Capt.
Robinson, Mr. Cater, and Rogers Ruding,
Esq. In the market-place, the great house,
the King's-head, and the building ad-
joining, are spacious; the house of Mrs.
Chambers, late Bailey's, in the Morlege;
in Iron-gate, that of John Newton, Esq.
Full-street boasts the house of Mr. Bing-
ham's, late lord Exeter's, once graced
with the presence of the unfortunate Prince
Charles; also the house of Dr. Darwin*;
in St. Mary-gate is the elegant residence
of Thomas Evans, Esq. that of the late
Hugh Bateman, Esq. and in Queen-

* For an account of this eminent Resident at
Derby, see Chalmers's Biographical Dictionary,
vol. XI. p. 286; or Davies's Derbyshire, p. 224.

EDIT.

street,

street, that of Mr. Latuffier; but the most superb is that of John Gisborn, Esq. in Bridge-gate, a house that would honour the first orders of Nobility, but in a situation which does not merit a dwelling of £.500. Wherever we find so expensive a work, we may fairly conclude the proprietor was either very rich, or did not dread poverty. There is one solitary mansion, however, which I cannot behold without a sigh: it was once the most eminent in Derby, but now ruined by time, and seems to mourn the loss of its master: it is called *Babington-hall*, and stands at the extremity of the lane of that name; both were derived from the ancient and opulent family of Babington of Dethick, one of the first in the county, which erected the building many centuries ago, and made it their residence. The last of this unfortunate race was Anthony Babington, who lost his life for adhering to the unhappy Mary Queen of Scots against Elizabeth. The family and the fortune sunk with him!—fallen greatness excites tender emotions!—one false step destroys the

growth

growth of ages! Though this venerable antique has, perhaps, experienced as many mutations as years, and is multiplied into half a dozen tenements, yet the original taste and grandeur of its Master are easily traced. The emblematical carvings are numerous, and in high perfection. In the last century this was the residence of Sir Simon Degge.

The country about Derby is delightful: the town is handsome. Camden calls it " an elegant place;" but some of the streets are narrow, dark, and dangerous. Improvements have, however, recently taken place, by accommodating the foot passenger with a pavement of flag-stones, if that can be deemed an accommodation which is too confined to allow two people to pass each other: neither does it amount to half a cure; for, as the streets have been narrow during the last two thousand years, they will probably continue so two thousand to come.

PUBLIC

PUBLIC BUILDINGS.

BRIDGES.

As the Derwent runs *by*, rather than *through* Derby, one bridge is sufficient, to which all the Eastern roads point. But as Markeaton brook passes *through* the place, the communication was preserved by ten; four paltry ones of stones, and six, more paltry, of timber: none of them passable in a flood; the three first are of timber upon Nuns-green; the fourth, stone, at Cuckstool-mill; a fifth at Bold-lane, timber; Warburgh's bridge, stone; the seventh, plank, upon a foundation of stone; which proves that the whole were of the same materials in the days of the Monk; this joins St. James's-lane to the Wardwick; the eighth, sixty yards below, plank; Jail bridge, now St. Peter's, stone; and Tenantbridge, a corruption of Tenth, in the Morlege, the same. Those of timber were designed

signed for foot people; the others were so ill constructed as scarcely to admit a horse with safety.

To the honour, however, of the present generation, they have recently taken down Cuckstool, Warburgh's, and the Jail bridges; and displayed their public spirit in erecting three in their places, more commodious than grand. Owing to these improved passages, two wretched bridges are destroyed as useless, the fifth and the eighth. There is yet room for a display of genius and accommodation in constructing Tenant-bridge, which calls loudly for the plan, the pick-axe, and the trowel.

To preserve a passage over Bramley brook, was a something which bore the name of *Pack-saddle-bridge*, from its shape; over which the traveller forbore to ride, except he chose to hazard a limb. This vile obstruction is also removed, and a convenient bridge placed in its stead.

All the Authors that ever wrote upon Derby are lavish with encomiums upon the beauty and elegance of *St. Mary's Bridge*, which

which is a proof they never saw it. Contradiction is an irksome task; but truth demands it. Its praise arises from its extraordinary elevation, which is one of its greatest defects: it is an arch upon arches; a mountain erected upon a river. Human infirmity, and loaded carriages, drag up heavily; but all move over it dangerously, being so extremely narrow as to admit but one carriage; so that we may safely remark, it cannot be travelled two ways at once. The gravel is incessantly washed away, owing to the steep ascent, and the arches left naked. Perhaps a bridge over so cold a river, so much used, and so ill adapted for use, cannot be found.

There is no evil without its good; if the stranger travels with difficulty to the summit of this bridge, he is well paid for his journey: the prospect is most charming; surprize and pleasure possess his mind; which, being ingrossed by the view, pass unobserved. Above the bridge the river gently winds, and moves on in solemn majesty; below he is delighted with the expansion,

pansion, the rustic island, the cascades, formed by the wears, as if art meant to confine this vast mass of water; but it spurns the confinement with dignity, and, like man, rejoices in liberty. The garden of ever-greens in the centre of the stream, the verdant meadows on the left, bounded by distant woods; the superb appearance of the Silk-Mills, All Saints, and other capital buildings, terminated by a varied and extensive prospect, please his eye, and engage his mind. He views, and would still view, but that he has a life to guard, in continual danger from the carriages, owing to the narrowness of the bridge.

About a century ago, this bridge demanding repairs, the mechanic head of Roger Morlege endeavoured to come at the foundation, by cutting a trench through the South end of the first field leading to Chester, and also the Nottingham road, and directing the stream down a lane on the right into its own bed near the Holmes. To accomplish this airy, or rather watery project, he drove piles quite across the bed
of

of the river, about two yards asunder, and twenty above the bridge. He then produced a wooden box, a yard wide, as high as the depth of the water, and long as the width. This was to be placed in the front of the piles as a barricade to the stream. The cumbrous machine, to make it sink, and act as a complete dam, was filled with earth; but the sullen water, fond of its old course, crept through the crannies as fast as they could drain it out. As the pride of man cannot brook a conquest, the box was taken up, and Roger, like Noah, pitched it within and without. This was to insure success; but the River proved as obstinate as Roger, would submit to no controul, but, regardless of the little efforts of man, moved on with its wonted majesty; and the project was given up with reluctance. The piles, I believe, are yet standing: I have seen them in a clear and low water.

At what time the present bridge was erected is uncertain; perhaps it has stood more than 300 years. To the honour of
the

C. Moneypenny Delin. *R. Hancock F.*

South View of the New Bridge over River Armount.

OF DERBY. 31

the present day, an Act and four thousand pounds are procured to erase that nuisance, which, for ages, has borne the epithet of *grand*, and to erect another bridge*ten yards above the present; but, I doubt, upon too small a scale. The people of Derby, like those of every other place, rest satisfied with an improvement *half* accomplished. They lose sight of an old, but excellent, adage, *Once well done is twice done;* nor is a useful hint remembered, which Lord Chesterfield drops to his Son, " If a thing be worth doing *at all*, it is worth doing well."

I could give as many intances of this short-sighted conduct as would fill a volume. I have known the pavement of a street taken up to lay it a little lower; and soon after taken up again to lay it still a *little* lower. I have known the hedges on both sides of a road demolished to widen it; and a few years after again removed to add more width.

* A new bridge of three arches has accordingly been erected. EDIT.

COUNTY HALL,

OR

COURT OF JUSTICE,

situate at the bottom of St. Mary-gate; erected in 1660, of free stone. The masonry was done by —————— *Reeve*, who saved nothing by the undertaking; but drank the profits as they sprang up; and the carpentry by Robert Morlege, father to him who attempted to curb the Derwent, and who was said to have acquired as much as erected his house at the bottom of St. Helen's-walk, since the residence of his family. It stands in a recess, as public buildings ought; and has a walk of flagstones, once graced with an avenue of trees, leading to the entrance; it still is handsome and convenient; it was long the pride of the Midland Circuit; longer the dread of the criminal and the client; but the delight of the lawyer. Were two evils cured, we should yet behold an accomplished piece of architecture: remove one house which

South View of the County Hall.

North View of the Town Hall

stands towards the East, and it would open the *whole* front; and eight vases placed upon the summit would relieve the heavy effect of the cornice.

GUILDHALL.

The spirit, riches, and taste of a people, are known by their public buildings. If the inhabitants are poor, indolent, or tasteless, they are apt to take up with *makeshifts*. I could instance a place which contains 60,000 people, 10,000 houses, 170 streets, and commands six millions, whose general meetings are held, and their public business is transacted, in a pitiful bed-chamber!

Derby must have had a succession of Guildhalls for many ages; but two only come under the pen. The last stood upon the same spot as the present; I knew it well; it seemed to have stood more than 200 years: it was wood and plaster; the roof was tiled, in the form of a large old-fashioned span; it had two stories;

the lower was called the Town-prison, and was divided into cells, as all prisons ought, that two rogues may not communicate their vices; the upper was a large room for corporation use, to which the company ascended by a steep flight of wooden stairs projecting into the market-place, and covered with a roof of tiles. The hall, the stairs, the conduit, and the cross, then in being, nearly choaked up the little market-place.

In 1730 this venerable building was taken down, and the present hall erected, which is an honour, a beauty, and a use.

It would surprize the stranger, that the buildings in the Leather-lane were not purchased, and the hall placed upon that spot, to range with the houses, or rather fallen back into a recess. This would have enlarged the market-place, and satisfied the eye. The proprietor, however, of those buildings was applied to, and offered an extravagant price; but as he knew the Corporation could go to no other market, he asked one more extravagant. Astonished

South East View of the Free School.

nished at the enormous sum, they refused the purchase, and began to build, when he sunk his price to theirs; but it was now too late. Thus a lasting benefit was sacrificed to a present profit! What pity the Corporation did not suffer themselves to be bit by extortion, rather than place the fabrick where it now stands, which is rendered, by its situation, a *disgusting* beauty!

Should Fortune ever give them power to remove that range, comprehending the Piazzas, Shambles, and Rotten Row, though it will not make the largest market-place in the kingdom, it will the most beautiful; and they will merit the thanks of posterity.

FREE SCHOOL.

It is curious to observe the mutation of property; like the tide, it is ever changing; sometimes it flows in abundance; and again retreats into want. From a multitude of people who expected eternal happiness, by depriving the future owners of what they could no longer enjoy themselves, Derley Abbey accumulated immense riches : families starved, while the abbey flourished. But from a plenitude of power, urged by an ungovernable appetite, Henry the Eighth seized the whole monastic property ; and now, the tide taking a contrary turn, families became rich by the seizure ; for Henry did not rob for himself, but others. Many of the donations belonging to Derley Abbey fell into the hands of the Corporation of Derby: with a small portion of these they erected a *Free School* in St. Peter's church-yard, and endowed it with lands set apart for the use. The profits then maintained two masters, at the annual income of £6. 13s. 4d. each. Time having augmented the value of landed property, the receipts are now £90. which supports two masters, one of £60. and the other of £30.

PRISONS.

Four prisons, in so small a place as Derby, would induce the stranger to suppose it a place of rascals! but, to the honour of the inhabitants, they are often empty. A slender prison indicates that the arts of governing are understood. Rogues are more frequently made by defective government in others, than in themselves. A wise legislator will rather nip an evil in the bud, than suffer it to grow to magnitude. If idleness be the nurse of crimes, employment must have a contrary effect. A proper regulation of diet, solitude, and work, will effect the cure of a culprit, when nothing else will.

Two of these prisons are jails; and two, houses of correction; one of each for the use of the town, under the jurisdiction of the Mayor; the other for the county, under that of the Sheriff. If they excite that terror in the mind which is productive of innocence, they answer a valuable purpose.

pose. A man whom I personally knew, rather defective in his intellects, played upon a rusty fiddle from house to house for a livelihood: but, as the law prohibits the use of the fiddle-stick on Sunday, he solicited charity at the church-door: the officer seized him, and shut him up in a garret, in the house of correction, joining the county hall. But he, like a true-born Englishman, impatient of confinement, attempted to jump out of the window; when, repenting one moment too late, he hung, for another moment, by a tile, when I saw both fall together into the County Hall-yard. Thus in ten minutes he found, and left, the prison empty. A crowd, full of compassion, instantly surrounded him, and blamed the officer for the seizure, who had certainly done no more than his duty, for a common beggar ought never to be suffered in the streets; if he is able to work, let him be constrained; if not, let the community support him. If the officer committed an error, it was in neglecting to bar his

window;

window; but he never suspected a man, who had lost his liberty without being criminal, would take a three-story leap to recover it. The unhappy man received an injury in his back, and afterwards became crooked.

Exclusive of these two houses of correction for small offenders, there is what is called *The Town Prison;* this, as observed, was under the old Town-hall. After that was destroyed, a small erection was added to the county prison, at the Jail Brook, which bore that name. Here in 1731 I saw the Jailor himself, John Greatrex, confined a prisoner for playing at foot-ball, a sport which the Mayor, Isaac Borrow, was determined to suppress. But the man, who had often confined others, could not brook confinement himself; he declared, in anger, "the prison should not hold him one night." He fulfilled his declaration; for he broke it, and fled before morning. This place of confinement is upon Nuns-green.

It

It is an old remark, that "the present generation is wiser than the last;" this is verified in the chief prison, or jail, at Derby. Our ancestors erected one in a river, exposed to damp and filth, as if they meant to drown the culprit before they hanged him. A worse situation could not have been chosen: it extended across the corn-market, one of the principal streets, or as if to hide the brook, or bind the flood. The wretched inhabitant was open to the public, and they to him. A vile arch admitted the horse passenger, and a viler the foot; inconvenient to both, hurtful to the stranger, dangerous to the inmate; a reflection upon the place, without one benefit as a counterbalance.—But their wiser successors destroyed this ancient reproach, of some centuries standing; and erected an elegant prison upon Nuns-green in 1756. Here the culprit enjoys light, air, and water, which ought never to be denied even the offender. The town has the credit of a handsome and suitable edifice; the Duke of Devonshire the pleasure

OF DERBY. 41

sure of contributing £400. towards the erection; and the traveller is delighted with the object.

ALMS HOUSES.

The word *Charity* is one of the most common in the English language, but few are less understood. Indiscriminately to *give* is not charity; nor is it charity to give to him that wants, if that want arises from himself. He who can earn a supply, and will not, it is no charity to relieve. To encourage him to labour who is unwilling, but must subsist by labour, is charity. To support infants who have none to help them; old age, even after a life of imprudence; or the afflicted, in any age, is charity. Charity may extend its influence even to youth and health; as when a young widow is left with children whom she is unable to support. Another species of charity, is the preparing an asylum for distress; but even *this* requires a judgement to distinguish objects, and a resolution

42 THE HISTORY

tion in the choice. There are three of this description in Derby, which bear the name *Alms-houses;* one is the Devonshire, near All Saints, erected by the famous Countess of Shrewsbury in the reign of Queen Elizabeth, for eight men and four women. Each hath two rooms, coals, and two shillings and sixpence per week : they wear dark cloaks badged with *E. S.* (Elizabeth Shrewsbury) on a silver plate. The building was of stone, which would have stood the blasts of 500 years to come : the windows small, according to the fashion of the day, which scarcely admitted the light. The present Duke took down this antique building, and erected the present upon a model perfectly new : instead of that modest elegance, which ought to have dignified the front, we should suppose it a Publick-office, a receptacle for Magistracy, or a place to study the Sciences. Who dresses a pauper in lace! We are treated with an ostentatious display of the Duke's arms and crest as leading objects. Thus the left hand perfectly

knows

C. Montgenny, Delin.   *West View of the Devonshire Alms House.*   *R. Hancock sc.*

South View of the Black Hospital.

knows what is done by the right.—That charity which longs to publish itself, ceases to be charity.

In this place we behold with pleasure that orderly race, whose ability just supported them through life, find a retreat when that ability fails. The statutes, to be observed by this venerable society, are some of them excellent, and some whimsical. They are ratified at entrance by a solemn oath, too strict to be kept: they cannot marry, nor get drunk, without expulsion; to lie out one night incurs a forfeiture of four-pence; to miss prayers at All Saints, two-pence; to be absent one day, sixpence; to strike a blow, one shilling; and three blows, a discharge.

The next are those in Bridge-gate, for the aged, called *The Black Alms-houses*, from the black-gown worn by the inhabitant; but they might, with equal propriety, be so called from the building, which is nearly as black as the gown; there are eight, for an equal number of each sex; they have eighteen-pence a week. This

foundation

foundation was laid by the family of Wilmot, of Chaddesdon, 200 years ago, who appropriated £40. *per ann.* for its support, charged upon the Tythes of Denby, which for many years fell short, and was made up by the family; but by the reduction of money, an overplus arises, to which the family have a right. Thus the eighteen-pence supported the ancient inhabitant a whole week, but now about two days.

Another set of five are at the top of Friar-gate, for the Widows of Clergymen. They were instituted in 1716 by Edward Large, of Derby, who endowed them with an estate which produces to each resident £17. *per ann.* The building is elegant; but injured by a puff of pride in the front of *Gloria soli Dei;* but the chief glory of the founder would have consisted in silence.—That religion issues from pride which a man exhibits to the public eye from his garret-window.

Perhaps this institution is one of the first species of charity we know; for as
those

Alms Houses for the Widows of Clergymen

those who never experienced plenty can never regret its loss, so poverty after affluence, coming with double effect, merits double compassion.

Charitable institutions, like men, have their rise, their meridian, decline, and extinction; and, like them, are cut off in a short, or protracted to a longer, day.— A fourth charity of the class we are describing, was called *The Grey-coat Hospital*, from the colour of the garment. This was situated in Walker's lane, and supported by ample endowments.—If the founder intended to perpetuate his name, or the wretched pauper expected an asylum, at the close of life, both are disappointed, for the inhabitant is gone, the building destroyed, and the estate vanished; as will ever be the fate of valuable property when unprotected.—Thus the expiring saint, who is climbing to heaven upon his own charities, had better consign his property to his next of kin, than turn it adrift to wreck upon the wide ocean of Fraud.

INFIRMARY.

INFIRMARY.

"The Derbyshire General Infirmary is situated a little way out of the town, on the South side near the London road. The ground on which it stands was purchased of the Corporation of Derby, at the price of £.200 an acre. The situation is elevated, airy, and dry, abounding with excellent water, and accessible by a good road. The design of the building was arranged by William Strutt, Esq. and the working plans were drawn by Mr. Browne. The building is constructed of a beautiful hard and durable whitish stone, of a cubical form, with an handsome elevation. It is three stories high, and well arranged; being able to accommodate eighty patients, besides those with infectious disorders. It was opened June 4, 1810. The expence of the land and erection of the Infirmary amounted to £.17,870. 3s. 4d. The donations amounted to £31,238. 19s. so that the balance, constituting the funds of the Infirmary, amounted to £.13,368. 15s. 8d."*

* Davies's " History of Derbyshire," p. 239.

OF DERBY. 47

ORDNANCE DEPOT.

" Not far from the Infirmary, and about the same distance from the town, is the *Ordnance Depot.* The ground on which this building stands, being an acre and a quarter, was purchased for the purpose by the Board of Ordnance in the year 1803. The respective buildings, erected according to a plan by Mr. Wyatt, the Architect, were completed in 1805. These consist of an Armory in the centre: the room on the ground-floor, being seventy-five feet long by twenty-five broad, is calculated to contain fifteen thousand stand of arms; these are disposed here in the same order as those are in the Tower of London, and present a very pleasing appearance, on the entrance to the room.—Above this is a room of the same proportions, containing accoutrements for the use of the army. On the North and South sides of the armory, are two magazines, capable of containing 1200 barrels of ammunition. These

are

are internally arched with brick, to prevent accidents; and, for the same purpose, conductors have been erected at a little distance from each. Four dwellings are situated in the angles of the exterior wall; two of which are Barracks for a detachment of Royal Artillery, and the other two, are the residence of Officers in the Civil Department of the Ordnance. Besides these buildings, suitable workshops, &c. have been erected on the inside of the surrounding wall. The establishment is under the superintendance of an Ordnance Storekeeper, who is appointed by the Master-General of the Ordnance.*"

ASSEMBLY.

The love of pleasure is the general attendant of youth, which knows well how to enjoy it. The love of profit is the attendant of age, which is defective in that knowledge. Here the order of things seems inverted. It appears more reasonable for

* Davies's "Derbyshire," p. 244—246.

young

West View of the Assembly House.

young persons to covet money, who, having life before them, may want it: but it can be of no use to the man who is entering the grave. There is, however, in this paradox a propriety. Were youth as fond of wealth as old age, the world would be pestered with a generation of misers, to the stagnation of property, and the injury of the community; for riches, like the sea, should ever fluctuate. But there can be no evil in placing them in the possession of an old man, because he is unable to keep them. It is only a bauble put into the hands of the child while it drops asleep.

For the recreation of youth there were two Assembly-rooms; to the pleasures of which age had no pretence; both at the bottom of Full-street; but as one was much the genteelest, it robbed the other of its votaries. The present elegant building, to which the Duke of Devonshire liberally contributed, fronts the Market-place, is of stone, begun in 1763, and completed by subscription in 1774; the pediment is adorned with musical instruments figurative of its use.

THEATRE.

The exhibitions of the Stage were held in a room in Iron-gate till 1773, when a convenient theatre was erected in Bold-lane, more striking than the street in which it stands.

WORKHOUSE.

It is but within memory that workhouses were established, which, from their name, indicate a place for labour. The design was an asylum for distress, and a cure for the beggar. But this is one instance, amongst many, of the weakness of human foresight: these have augmented the evil they were intended to reduce. Workhouses, in a small degree, are beneficial, as being a temporary home for the disorderly and friendless, who have none of their own; a retreat for the prostitute, furnished with powers to taint the world and destroy herself. All these characters ought to be
initiated

West View of the Church.

initiated into labour, till another home and employment can be found.—But, according to the present mode of conducting workhouses, they are completely destructive; they are the nurseries of idleness, the corrupters of manners, the receptacles of vulgarity, the sinks of rudeness, the destroyers of health, the slaughter-houses of infants, and the plagues of old age: if there be a hell upon earth, as taught by our old nurses, it must be in a crowded prison, where corruptions grow with hasty shoots: if there be a purgatory, as taught by a venerable church, many of whose adherents I esteem, it must be in a workhouse, where order is routed by discord.

A workhouse should never be without a manufactory; but we find it in very few. Neither is there any place in which labour is more detested. What man will work if he can be supported without! If we seek for health, are we likely to succeed in a family consisting of some scores, if not some hundreds, of the lowest class, and most of them companions of filth! How can the tender

tender infant prosper in such horrid soil! perhaps not one in ten of these innocent and lovely plants rises to maturity! Age and infirmity seek repose; but in a workhouse they seek in vain: no eye to pity, no hand to help; brow-beaten by the governor, and hunted by the rude, they find repose only in the grave. Inimical to the natural freedom of man, the workhouse is neither more or less than a prison, and often of the most detrimental kind; consequently, it carries a degree of punishment which ought never to attend the innocent. The man of fair character, who has raised a family by industry, without being able to save a shilling for old age; the indisposed, who have neither friends or property; and the unhappy widow, left with unfortunate infants; can never be the objects of punishment.

The present use of workhouses is the most expensive mode of supporting the poor. It was the practice of some overseers to *fill* the house; it was mine to thin it; and the quantum of levies shewed which
was

was right. A pauper, once admitted, will never depart till he can carry out a better dress than he carried in. They are places ill adapted for the cure of disease. No consumptive person should ever enter, or infant be born, except they are designed for destruction; both should be sent to nurse, and that in a better air than is ever breathed in a workhouse.

There are five parishes in Derby, and four workhouses, St. Michael's being too small to require one*. They seem tolerably clean, and conducted in as orderly a manner as such receptacles usually are. The use of tobacco should be allowed.

	Persons.
In that of All Saints are about	63
St. Peter's	42
St. Warburgh's	32
and St. Alkmund's	30

The poor's-rates amount to about one tenth of the annual rents.

* This parish also has now a workhouse. EDIT.

EARLS

EARLS OF DERBY.

Titles, like shoes, are subject to alter with use; the more they are worn, the less their value. Power and title were formerly united in partnership; but now their union is dissolved, and their influence reduced.

The title of *Duke* was always annexed to sovereignty, as those of Burgundy, Normandy, Savoy, and Tuscany. This title was unknown in England till Edward the Third conferred it upon his son, the Black Prince, by creating him Duke of Cornwall. Here we find it in a subject; since which it has dwindled merely to a sound.—That of Earl also, the only title left us by the Saxons, was borne by princes, as those of Flanders, Hainault, &c. And though under our Saxon ancestors they were subjects, yet their power was great, little inferior to that of royalty: but now they are only titular, a name without a substance, a winter's sun without power.

Derby,

Derby, in the compass of 650 years, has given this title to four potent families; that of Ferrers, in which it continued eight descents; Plantagenet, one; another branch of Plantagenet, three; and Stanley, twelve. The first had prodigious power and property in the place united to the title; the second and third had less; and the fourth has none.

Henry de Ferrers came over with the Conqueror, and settled at Tutbury Castle.

1. His grandson Robert, in 1138, having great interest in Derbyshire, raised a powerful force; and, with other Northern chiefs, opposed and defeated David King of Scots at Northallerton, while King Stephen was absent. For this service the King created him Earl of Derby; but he enjoyed the title only one year.

2. His son Robert succeeded him in 1139, performed many pious works, among which was that of erecting St. Helen's, in Derby; he also built and endowed the Abbey of Merry-vale, near Atherston; and ordered his body to be wrapped in an ox's hide and interred there.

3. William

3. William his son succeeded in 1147. He held 203 lordships, of which 114 were in Derbyshire. The male line of the Peverels did not continue more than four descents; the last of which, William, left a daughter, Margaret, whom this William de Ferrers married, and received with her a vast fortune of the Peverels, which joining to his own, he became immensely rich. Among other property he enjoyed the third penny arising from tolls, trials, forfeitures, &c. which had passed from the Earls of Mercia to the Peverels; the other two pennies being the claim of the Crown.

4. Robert, his son, inherited his title and property; and, after a life without effect, died in 1173, the 19th of Henry II.

5. William, his son, succeeded. He rebelled against Henry the Second; and also against his successor, Richard the First: but, being on the weaker side, was deprived of his honours and estates.

Richard then conferred upon his brother, John Plantagenet, the earldom and castles of Nottingham, Lancaster, and Derby,
with

with the honour of Peverel. But, John soon after mounting the throne, the lustre of the title, like a candle in the sun, was lost in that of the crown.

This William de Ferrers, the fifth Earl, died in 1191.

6. His son William being in favour with John, the King created him Earl of Derby by special charter at Northampton. He was girt with a sword by the King's own hand, being the first so created. His third penny, enjoyed by the Saxon Earls, with other property, was restored. The next year King John granted him the service of William de Gresley, and his heirs, for his lands at Drakelow, to hold by the annual payment of a bow, quiver, and twelve arrows.

He also granted him, June 27, in the fifteenth year of his reign, a house in the parish of St. Margaret, London, which was Isaac's the Jew of Norwich; to be held of the King and his heirs, on condition that Ferrers and his heirs should serve before the King and his heirs at dinner, at all annual

annual and other feasts, with his head uncovered; except that he should have on a garland the breadth of the little finger of him or his heirs: and this was to be for all service.

He died in 1247, 31st of Henry the Third, after spending the prime of his life at the political helm; and the latter end in endowing monasteries.

7. William succeeded; and passed his time in improving his estate, already too large for one man to conduct. He was well versed in the laws of his country, as every gentleman ought to be. Thus the father recovered the ancient lustre of the family, and the son preserved it. Being too much afflicted with the gout to use his feet, he rode in a chariot; and, by the carelessness of the driver, was overturned in passing the bridge at St. Noat's, and killed in 1254. He was interred with his ancestors at Merry-vale.

8. Robert, his son, was a minor. When at maturity, he joined the Barons against Henry the Third: young, rich, and spirited,

he

he marched with his soldiers into Worcester, destroyed a place called the Jury, plundered the religious and private houses, and ruined the King's parks.—Henry sent his son, afterwards Edward the First, with an army to destroy the Earl's estates in the counties of Stafford and Derby, where he retaliated the injury with sword and fire; a poor revenge upon the innocent!

After the battle of Evesham, where he fought under Mountfort, he was excluded the liberty of redeeming his estate by a fine of five years purchase, granted to all, except a very few. He afterwards found means of purchasing his pardon; but not being able to keep his factious temper within bounds, he not only omitted paying the price agreed on, but raised an army in Derbyshire to oppose the King; who sent against him his nephew, Henry, Prince of Allemagne. Robert was defeated, and hid himself under some sacks of wool in a church; but, being discovered by a woman, was brought a prisoner to London: his title was forfeited,

forfeited, his estate confiscated, and himself confined a prisoner three years.

Henry bequeathed the chief of this property to his own son, Edmund Plantagenet, known by the name of Cruch-back: but the boisterous Robert found means again to work upon the fickle Henry; for in the 53d of his reign it was agreed, that Edmund should resign to the Earl all his property, in consideration of being paid, at one payment, £.50,000 upon a day fixed. Robert could as soon have raised the dead as this enormous sum, a sum nearly equal to the value of a county; nay, the cash in currency would scarcely have furnished it. He procured, however, several able securities for payment: as Henry, son to Richard, King of the Romans; the Earls of Pembroke, Warren, Surrey, Warwick, Roger de Someri, Thomas de Clare, Robert Walraund, Roger de Clifford, Hammand le Strange, Bartholomew de Sudley, and Robert de Briwer, all great barons. Perhaps this was the most illustrious set of private bondsmen ever known. The Earl, as a
counter

counter security, assigned nearly all his estate, keeping Chartley and Holbrook. But the money, as might have been expected, was never paid; and Robert never recovered his title or property. This was in 1265, after the Ferrers's had enjoyed the Earldom 127 years; and the estate from the Conquest, being 199.——Here we behold the fallacy of human possessions! The folly of that solicitude often beheld in a father to promote the future grandeur of his son! The Ferrers's estate was immense; and the father of this Robert was studious to augment it; but the son, in a small space, destroyed the work of ages. If a fortune of millions cannot last one short life, what then will become of a few thousands when in the hands of Imprudence! This idea will administer consolation to the man who leaves his descendants naked.

Several members of the House of Lords are the offspring of this ancient and illustrious family; as Shirley, Earl Ferrers; Lord Hereford; the late Lord Huntingdon; Lord de Ferrers; the Duke of Northumberland;

thumberland; and even the Royal Family. The Corporation of Derby pays the Earl of Essex £.16 *per ann.* as a fee farm rent; being a commutation, which has been fixed for ages, in lieu of the third penny mentioned above, granted by the Crown 600 years ago to Ferrers, from whom he is also descended.

The prosperity of this ancient family being cut off by misconduct, the title lay dormant 64 years, till 1329, the second of Edward the Third, who created,

1. Henry Plantagenet, Earl of Derby, son to Henry Earl of Lancaster, son to Edmund Cruch-back, second son of Henry the Third. This Earl of Derby had a daughter, Blanch, who married,

2. John of Gaunt; and brought with her the Earldom.

3. Henry, her son, inherited it in her right till he mounted the throne, under the title of Henry the Fourth, when the honour of Derby again slept in the Crown till 1485, when Henry the Seventh conferred it upon,

1. Thomas Lord Stanley, of Knocking,

in

in the county of Lancaster. The founder of this illustrious race came over as an officer in the army of William the First, under the name of *Audley;* whose descendant, Nicholas de Audley, was created by Edward the First, in 1296, Baron Audley, of Highleigh, in the county of Stafford. This honour became extinct in 1391. One of the family being proprietor of the manor of Stanley, in the county of Derby, took it for his surname, the practice of that day.— John, the seventh in descent from him who assumed the name of Stanley, married Isabella, heiress of the house of Latham, by which he acquired a vast fortune. Richard the Second made him Lord Deputy and Lord Lieutenant of Ireland; and Henry the Fourth made him Steward of his Household, and also conferred upon him the *royalty of Man.* Such were the effects of a happy conduct, which could conciliate the affections of contending Kings. Henry the Sixth created him Baron Stanley of Latham in 1456. He died in 1459. To him succeeded his son, the above Thomas Stanley

of

of Knocking, the first Earl of Derby. He married Eleanor, daughter of Richard Neville Earl of Salisbury, and sister to the great Earl of Warwick. He had several sons by this marriage. George, the eldest, married Jane, heiress of Lord Strange, who carried into the Stanley family the title and fortune: this George was the person whom Richard the Third required as an hostage for the fidelity of his father. Thomas, the first Earl, while Lord Stanley, was in favour with Edward the Fourth, who made him Steward of his Household. He was renowned for arms; commander of the right wing of that army which Edward sent against Scotland under his brother the Duke of Gloucester. He married, for his second wife, Margaret Countess of Richmond, who, with her son, afterwards Henry the Seventh, were the only remaining heirs of the line of Lancaster: this alliance was without issue. He was a firm adherent to Edward the Fifth; for which Richard the Third intended to have dispatched him, as if by accident, at the council-board, when Hastings fell.

Richard,

Richard, however, having carried the Crown, endeavoured to win his affections by making him Steward of his Household, and Lord High Constable of England for life: but Lord Stanley, justly supposing the man who designed to take his life could never be his friend, threw his whole weight into Richmond's scale, in whose favour he drew a successful sword at Bosworth-field, seized the crown of Richard, and placed it upon the brow of Henry. Henry in return gave him the Earldom of Derby. He died in 1504, and was buried in Burscough Priory. George, his eldest son, died sixteen years before him, 1488, and was buried at St. James's, Garlick-hithe, London. The title then fell to *his* son,

2. Thomas, grandson to the first Earl. He died in 1521, and lies in Sion Abbey.

3. Edward succeeded; was in favour with Henry the Eighth, Edward the Sixth, Mary, and Elizabeth; and is celebrated by the Historians for beneficence and hospitality. He died in 1572, and was buried at Ormskirk.

4. Henry,

4. Henry, his son, died in 1594; and his son,

5. Ferdinand enjoyed the honour but one year, and left it without issue in 1595.

6. William, his brother, inherited the honours; and, dying in 1642, was succeeded by his son,

7. James, a steady friend to the House of Stuart. Oliver in vain offered him his own terms, if he would deliver up the Isle of Man. With twelve hundred men he encountered, near Wigan, three thousand under Col. Lilborn for two hours, was defeated, after receiving seven musket-shot on his breast-plate, thirteen blows with the sword upon his helmet, five wounds upon his body, and having two horses killed under him. He was taken in the pursuit after the battle of Worcester, September 3, 1651, and suffered decapitation at Bolton October 15; which was inflicted with marks of cruelty, his greatest crime being of that heinous nature which could not be forgiven, *power*. He married, in early life, Charlotte, daughter of Claude de la Tremouille, Duke of

of Thouors, and was blessed with a numerous issue. This gallant Lady has perpetuated her name in history by defending Latham house eighteen weeks, when besieged by the Parliament forces, not with the spirit of a man, but with that of a hero.

8. Charles, his son, succeeded. He enlisted some forces for Charles the Second during the insurrection of Sir George Booth in 1659, was taken prisoner, escaped punishment, and died in 1672.

9. William succeeded him, but died without male issue in 1702; when his brother,

10. James inherited the honour and estate; but left both without heirs in 1736. He served under King William in Flanders. Queen Anne made him Chancellor of the Duchy of Lancaster; and George the First, Captain of the Yeomen. At the death of this nobleman, the title devolved to,

11. Sir Edward Stanley, of Bickerstaff, the ninth in descent from the second son of George, eldest son of Thomas, who won the earldom at Bosworth-field. But the

the Royalty of Man passed as private property into the Athol family, by a female descendant from James, the seventh Earl, beheaded by Cromwell. This Edward died in 1776, at the age of 86; and was succeeded by,

12. Edward, his grandson, the present Earl, born in 1752; elected for Lancashire in 1774. When he came to the Earldom, he was made Lord Lieutenant and Custos Rotulorum for the county; in 1783, Chancellor of the Duchy and County Palatine of Lancaster. He married in 1774 Elizabeth, daughter of James, the seventh Duke of Hamilton, by the celebrated Miss Gunning; and amuses himself in the distribution of Twenty Thousand a year, in the cheerful bottle and the song, and in acquiring an election victory over the potboiling Corporation of Preston.

GOVERNMENT.

Man is a variegated animal. Left to himself, he will often do right, but oftener wrong.

wrong. Hence it becomes necessary, in all assemblages of men, whether they compose a kingdom, or a private family, to fabricate rules for the modification of action. These are the laws of society, instituted by general consent, for the security of the whole. Under a wise legislation, they are always founded in reason, and for their performance every member becomes a guarantee. This is order; without which, no community can prosper.

Though we are apt to treat the antient Britons as savages (for the living ever asperse the dead); yet many of their laws were less absurd than our own. The arts of government were understood; and the heavy legions of Cæsar might have been unsuccessful, had not unanimity fled from the Britons. Provincial government prevailed; and Derby was under the officers of the day, but of what denomination we are prevented from knowing by the infant state of letters.

While the Roman power existed, government wore a military aspect, and the sword directed the laws.

During

During the Heptarchy, the *Bailiff* was the commanding officer, and still continued to be so, after Egbert had reduced the kingdom into one sole monarchy. This officer was subject to the Reeve; and *he* to the Earl of Mercia, who himself held a kind of second-hand sovereignty under the Crown. In this period Derby was made a Royal Borough; that is, the private property of the Prince; but the exact time cannot be ascertained. It must, in that early age, have enjoyed many privileges by charter; for, in the reign of Edward the Confessor, 1040, Derby contained the amazing number of 243 burgesses or freemen, commanders of property, equal perhaps, in that day, to several thousand pounds in this. They held twelve ploughgates, as much lands as twelve teams usually ploughed in a year. Though the whole manor was open, every man knew his own; the meadow grounds being divided into doles, and the tillage by meers. The freemen possessed their land by a kind of copyhold right. The King, the Earl, and the

OF DERBY. 71

the Church, were the chief proprietors; and the exorbitant sum of £.24 was paid to the Crown as an annual rent. There is also said in this reign to have been fourteen corn mills in the town.

The chief part of the people were divided into two classes, *Freemen* and *Villans*; the latter were by far the most numerous. If we consider the great number of principal inhabitants, the still greater of the lower class, the many teams employed in their service, the great extent of houses and land, which could produce the astonishing rent of £.24. equal to the price of a manor (for land could not be worth one shilling an acre, nor a house five); and also, the prodigious number of corn-mills to feed the people; the place must have been, in that early age, large and flourishing, perhaps not less so than within memory.

The profits arising from tolls, customs, &c. were, as above, divided into three parts: two went to the King, and one to the Earl of Mercia. Thus serenity and
prosperity,

prosperity, which are the result of protection, attended Derby during the mild sunshine of Saxon influence, but alas! the season of darkness and horror was approaching!

In the reign of William the First, many of the houses were left desolate; more went to decay; their fourteen corn-mills were reduced to ten; their 243 burgesses were diminished to 140; and 40 of these were minors. This calamity, no doubt, arose from a change of government. Earl Edwin was rich and powerful: he was the friend of Harold, and of his Country; and when the King of Norway, accompanied by Earl Toston, invaded Northumberland, in 1066, Edwin raised his vassals, which thinned Derby, and, joining his forces with Morcard, another English nobleman, gave battle to the enemy before Harold could advance, but was defeated. When Harold arrived, he totally vanquished the Norwegian Monarch; but before he could well effect this, the Norman was landed, which obliged him instantly to travel from the

North

North into Sussex to face him; when, in their return through Derby, Edwin farther drained it, to recruit the army.—The day was lost! and though Edwin did not fall in battle, yet in trying to save a falling country, he fell himself. His followers lost their *all:* a hundred and three empty houses in Derby, going to decay, mourned the loss of their masters; and the lisping orphans seem to tell us, that their fathers were left in Battle field.

The Conqueror, being seated on the British throne, gave the property of the disinherited English to his followers. Derby, together with a prodigious rent-roll, was given to his illegitimate son, William Peverel, with nearly the same emoluments, as were enjoyed by the Mercian Earls. But as empty houses and neglected lands were ill adapted to pay levies, encouragement was given to population and industry by a new charter, with an augmentation of privileges and of rent; which last was raised to £.30 a year, and twelve thraves of corn, about 18 bushels;

out

out of which the Abbot of Burton had 40 sheaves, nearly five bushels; and, to balance the surcharge, Litchurch was added to the town. The two pennies to the King, and one to Peverel, were also continued.

Henry the First granted Derby to Ralph Earl of Chester; but, I suppose, during the minority only of a Peverel. He also incorporated the town by Charter, which is one of the first we know. It was altered and improved by Henry the Second, that father of freedom, who incorporated more places than any other English Prince. Richard the First improved the grant; so did John; but all new grants, like new leases, carried an advance of rent. In this reign the Corporation and Burgesses were sued in the Court of Exchequer for 66 marks, which they owed for rent, and for confirmation of their liberties; and again, in the sixth of his reign, for 60 marks, and two horses, for rent, and £.10 for services; and again, in the twelfth of his reign, for £.40.

Time and neglect are destructive to
sleeping

sleeping deeds, by which evidences are lost, and possessions endangered, especially if attacked by power. Whenever the Sovereign wanted money, he endeavoured to find it by raking into old charters. Edward the Third, in the ninth of his reign, deprived the Corporation of their liberties, and brought them into one of the King's Courts, and demanded " By what authority they took a toll, and paid none? Why they claimed the exclusive privilege of dying cloth, and prohibiting it in every other place within 30 miles, except Nottingham? By what authority they chose a Bailiff, and kept a fair on Friday in Whitsun - week; another at St. James, and held it seventeen days? What right they had to a Coroner; or, not to be sued out of their own borough? And why they kept a weekly market on Sunday, Monday, Wednesday, and Friday?"

It is curious to trace this catalogue of immunities to its source. The receipt of toll, and their own exemption throughout the King's dominions; the choice of a
Bailiff,

Bailiff, and the right of not being sued out of Derby, no doubt, arose from that Saxon Monarch who created it a Royal Borough; the exclusive liberty of dying cloth in Nottingham and Derby, from the interest of Peverel, who was lord of both; and the fairs, the coroner, and the market-days, from the subsequent charters of Saxon and Norman Kings. We may farther remark, a town must be of considerable magnitude to require four market-days; and that Sunday was not viewed in that sacred light it has since been.

In answer to these Exchequer accusations, the people of Derby produced some mutilated charters, but more arguments; some of them were powerful; but the most convincing was that of paying a fine of 40 marks, and consenting to an annual rent of £.46. 16s.

James the First, in 1611, granted a charter, which confirms those of former Kings; and adds, " That the Bailiffs, Recorder, and Town-clerk, shall keep a Court of Record, on Tuesday, every fortnight;
shall

shall be Justices of the Peace during office, and the following year; shall have the sole return of writs, keep a quarterly sessions, two court leets, six fairs, be toll free throughout the kingdom, and take toll from all, except the Duchy of Lancaster, which shall pay but half." These privileges remain.

Charles the First, in 1638, erected the Bailiff into a Mayor; but as there were two, Henry Mellor and John Hope, it was ordered, that the former should enjoy the honour, and his colleague succeed him; but, he dying in six months, Hope reigned the time of both; each had a mace; but, in 1660, they were thrown aside, and the present mace constructed.

The Corporation consists of ten Aldermen, including the Mayor; fourteen Brethren, out of whom the Aldermen are supplied; fourteen Common-Conncil, who rise into Brethren; a High-steward, who is the *Duke of Devonshire;* a Recorder, *William Fitzherbert,* Esq.; Town-clerk, *John Newton,* Esq.; and six Constables;
the

78 THE HISTORY

the last are annual. The Aldermen, according to seniority, are [1790],
> Thomas Eaton,
> William Edwards,
> Charles Heath,
> John Hope,
> Matthew How,
> Francis Ashby, Mayor,
> Samuel Crompton,
> Thomas Mather,
> Henry Flint,
> Benjamin Oldknow.

As a Corporate Body, they are possessed of about £.600. a year.

A LIST OF THE
BAILIFFS AND MAYORS

Derby must have been governed by a Bailiff in very early ages; but the time cannot be ascertained. The Corporation being unable to prove their right to a Bailiff, when sued in the King's Courts, 460 years ago, proves the great antiquity of this officer.

It

It was even then held by prescription, time having destroyed the original grant, which probably was part of the charter of Henry the First. No list can be found prior to the beginning of Henry the Eighth. Here we find the ancestors of many families still resident.

1513. John Brownhill, Thomas Bartholomew.
14. John Stringer, Christopher Thacker.
15. Robert Liversage, William Farrington.
16. Edward Walker, John Jepson.
17. James Oxeley, Roger Haye.
18. William Woodhouse, John Johnson.
19. Nicholas Orchard, Thomas Parr.
1520. Roger Moore, Thomas Walker.
21. Thomas Bartholomew, John Storrer.
22. Thomas Harnold, Thomas Parker.
23. Roger Smith, Hugh Walker.
24. Robert Liversage, John Brookhouse.
25. Robert Jepson, Oliver Thacker.
26. Robert York, Elias Cooper.
27. Nicholas Orchard, Roger Haye.
28. Roger Moore, Thomas Ward.
29. Richard Ilsley, Thomas Blockshaw.
1530. Thomas Bartholomew, John Storrer.
31. Thomas Walker, Thomas Parker.
32. Roger Smith, John Brookhouse.

1533.

1533. Robert Jepson, —— Johnson.
  34. Christopher Thacker, Robert York.
  35. Roger Haye, Elias Cooper.
  36. Thomas Parr, Thomas Ward.
  37. Thomas Ilsley, Thomas Blackshaw.
  38. Oliver Thacker, Robert Ragge.
  39. Thomas Parker, Richard Stringer.
1540. William Bradshaw, Edward Turner.
  41. William Allestry, William Hodgkinson.
  42. Robert Brookhouse, William Smith.
  43. Humphry Sutton, Edward Lenton.
  44. Thomas Ward, William Buckley.
  45. John Botham, John Alsop.
  46. Robert Ragg, Thomas Storrer.
  47. Richard Ward, Robert Smith.
  48. Richard Stringer, William Bradshaw.
  49. William Allestry, Richard Parkinson.
1550. John Wilson, William Fletcher.
  51. Richard Haye, Anthony Bate.
  52. Thomas Ward, Edward Garton.
  53. Oliver Thacker, Humphry Lutton.
  54. William Moore, Thomas Walker.
  55. Richard Ward, William Bembrigge.
  56. William Bradshaw, John Botham.
  57. James Thacker, Thomas Alsop.
  58. William Allestry, Richard Doughtye.
  59. Richard Parkinson, Ralph Bentley.
1560. Thomas Brookhouse, Robert Stringer.

1561. Henry York, Robert Turner.
  62. William Moore, Robert Watson.
  63. Richard Ward, William Bembrigge.
  64. William Aspinhall, Thomas Bate.
  65. Thomas Goulder, William Bradshaw.
  66. William Allestry, Anthony Bate.
  67. John Botham, Richard Doughty.
  68. Thomas Alsop, Richard Collier.
  69. Ralph Bentley, William Wandall.
1570. Thomas Brookhouse, Richard Harrison.
  71. Robert Stringer, Ralph Houghton.
  72. Henry York, Edward Bonsall.
  73. Robert Turner, Robert Greves.
  74. Robert Watson, Ralph Ballydon.
  75. William Bembrigge, Edward Turner.
  76. Thomas Bate, Thomas Walker.
  77. Thomas Goulder, Thomas Ilsley.
  78. William Allestry, Edward Fletcher.
  79. Richard Doughty, Thomas Campion.
1580. Ralph Bentley, Robert Wilmot.
  81. William Wandall, William Bolton.
  82. Robert Stringer, Henry Woxden.
  83. Ralph Haughton, Edmund Smith.
  84. Thomas York, Robert Wood.
  85. Edward Turner, Richard Fletcher, *Butcher.*

1586.

1586. Thomas Bate, William Bentley.
  87. Thomas Walker, Thomas Ilsley.
  88. Richard Doughty, Richard Fletcher, *Mercer*.
  89. Ralph Bentley, Thomas Campion.
1590. Robert Wilmot, William Botham.
  91. Robert Stringer, Thomas Fritch.
  92. Robert Wood, Robert Brookhouse.
  93. Edmund Turner, Edmund Smith.
  94. William Bentley, Edmund Sleigh.
  95. Thomas Walker, Elias Hawkes.
  96. Thomas Ilsley, John Parker.
  97. Robert Fletcher, Robert Brownell.
  98. William Botham, Nicholas Sleigh.
  99. Robert Stringer, James Osborn.
1600. Robert Wood, Richard Haughton.
   1. Robert Smith, Robert Bate.
   2. William Bentley, Richard Porter.
   3. Thomas Walker, Thomas Beck.
   4. Edward Sleigh, William Patter.
   5. John Parker, Peter Gery.
   6. Robert Brounell, William Wandall.
   7. Robert Wood, William Turner.
   8. Richard Haughton, Gervese Sleigh.
   9. Edmund Smith, Matthew Bate.
1610. William Bentley, Oliver Potter.
  11. Richard Potter, Thomas Fisher.

1612.

OF DERBY. 83

1612. Thomas Beck, William Walker.
13. Peter Gery, Robert Patter.
14. Richard Wandell, William Ward.
15. William Turner, Thomas Smith.
16. Matthew Bate, Thomas Goodwynne.
17. Thomas Fletcher, Thomas Stringer.
18. Oliver Potter, Henry Fisher.
19. Peter Geary, Edward Walker.
1620. Robert Patter, Samuel Parker.
21. William Turner, William Patter.
22. Thomas Smith, Nathaniel Halloms.
23. Francis Goodwynne, Wm. Bradshaw.
24. Thomas Fisher, William Francis.
25. Henry Wandall, Stephen Sleigh.
26. Henry Fisher, Thomas Walker.
27. Henry Mellor, Edward Walker.
28. William Potter, Edward Large.
29. Thomas Smith, John Hope.
1630. Nathaniel Hallows, Luke Whillington.
31. William Bradshaw, Thomas Haughton.
32. William Francis, Samuel Doughty.
33. Thomas Fisher, Francis Goodwynne.
34. Henry Wandall, Joseph Parker.
35. Stephen Sleigh, Robert Brookhouse.
36. Henry Fisher, Thomas Parker.
37. Henry Mellor, John Hope.

MAYORS.

MAYORS.

1638. Henry Mellor.
  39. John Hope.
1640. Edward Large.
  41. Luke Whillington.
  42. Henry Wandall.
  43. Luke Whillington.
  44. Luke Whillington.
  45. Gervase Bennet.
  46. John Dalton.
  47. Robert Mellor.
  48. Thomas Sleigh.
  49. Edward Large.
1650. John Parker.
  51. William Willot.
  52. John Dalton.
  53. Thomas Youle.
  54. Humphry Yates.
  55. Thomas Sleigh.
  56. Gilbert Ward.
  57. Nathaniel Halloms.
  58. Edward Large. He died, and John Parker served.
  59. John Gisborn.
1660. John Dunnidge.

1661.

1661. Thomas Patter.
  62. John Brookhouse.
  63. Edward Walker.
  64. Robert Wandall.
  65. John Harryman.
  66. Hugh Newton.
  67. Samuel Spateman.
  68. John Dalton.
  69. Humphry Yates.
1670. James Ward.
  71. John Spateman. He dying, Roger Newton supplied his place.
  72. Roger Newton.
  73. Thomas Goodwin.
  74. George Blackwell.
  75. Edward Walker.
  76. Samuel Spateman.
  77. John Brookhouse.
  78. Robert Wandell.
  79. Roger Newton.
1680. John Lord.
  81. Edward Walker.
  82. Roger Newton.
  83. Thomas Goodwin.
  84. John Dunnidge.
  85. Joseph Worden.
  86. Solomon Roberts.
1687.

1687. Leonard Sadd; discharged by James II. who put in Ralph Brough.
88. John Cheshire.
89. Samuel Spateman.
1690. Samuel Cheshire.
91. Samuel Fletcher.
92. John Lord.
93. Thomas Goodwin.
94. Henry Holmes.
95. Henry Noton.
96. Solomon Roberts.
97. William Francis.
98. Thomas Goodwin. Died, and Thomas Carter served.
99. William Francis.
1700. William Francis.
1. Thomas Carter.
2. Joseph Bloodworth.
3. Francis Cokayne.
4. William Turner.
5. Thomas Bott.
6. Joseph Broughton.
7. Thomas Byram.
8. John Holmes.
9. Thomas Fisher.
1710. Richard Ward.
11. Francis Cokayne.

1712.

1712. Thomas Gisborn.
13. Joseph Broughton.
14. Thomas Fisher.
15. Thomas Rivett.
16. John Bagnall.
17. Thomas Grey.
18. John Holmes.
19. Richard Ward.
1720. Hugh Bateman.
21. Francis Cokayne.
22. William Woolley.
23. Philip Parr.
24. Thomas Gisborn.
25. Samuel Cooper.
26. John Bagnall.
27. Thomas Houghton.
28. Robert Wagstaff.
29. John Gisborn.
1730. Isaac Borrow.
31. Nathaniel Edwards.
32. John Holmes.
33. Francis Cokayne.
34. Thomas Gisborn.
35. Samuel Cooper.
36. John Bagnall.
37. John Gisborn.
38. Robert Wagstaff.

1739.

1739. Robert Bakewell.
1740. Joshua Smith.
41. Samuel Fox.
42. Isaac Borrow.
43. Thomas Gisborn.
44. Samuel Cooper.
45. Robert Hague.
46. Humphry Booth.
47. Henry Francis; died, and Humphry Booth chosen.
48. Matthew How.
49. Thomas Gisborn.
1750. Joseph Bingham.
51. Robert Bakewell.
52. Humphry Booth.
53. Matthew How.
54. Robert Bakewell.
55. William Evans.
56. Robert Bakewell.
57. John Bingham.
58. Samuel Crompton.
59. Robert Bakewell.
1760. Joseph Bingham.
61. Thomas Rivett.
62. Thomas Milnes; died, and Joshua Smith served.
63. John Heath.

1764.

1764. Samuel Wilde.
  65. William Evans.
  66. Samuel Wilde.
  67. Samuel Crompton.
  68. William Evans.
  69. Thomas Stamford.
1770. Henry Flint.
  71. Thomas Eaton.
  72. John Heath.
  73. William Edwards.
  74. Christopher Heath.
  75. Robert Hope.
  76. William Leaper.
  77. Robert Hope. He died; and Samuel Crompton served the year out.
  78. Francis Ashby.
  79. Matthew Howe.
1780. William Edwards.
  81. John Hope.
  82. Samuel Crompton.
  83. Thomas Mather.
  84. Francis Ashby.
  85. William Edwards.
  86. Henry Flint.
  87. John Hope.
  88. Samuel Crompton.
  89. Thomas Mather.
1790.

1790. Francis Ashby.
91. Thomas Lowe.
92. John Crompton.
93. William Snowden.
94. Richard Leaper.
95. John Hope.
96. John Leaper Newton.
97. Rev. Charles Stead Hope.
98. William Edwards.
99. Henry Browne.
1800. John Crompton.
1. Samuel Rowland.
2. Thomas Lowe.
3. William Snowden.
4. John Hope.
5. Rev. Charles Stead Hope.
6. John Drewry.
7. Richard Leaper.
8. Henry Browne.
9. Samuel Rowland.
1810. John Crompton.
11. Thomas Haden.
12. Henry Lowe.
13. Thomas Lowe.
14. John Drewry.
15. Richard Leaper.
16. Rev. Charles Stead Hope.

MEMBERS
FOR THE
BOROUGH.

How long the people of England have been represented in the great council of the nation has never been determined by our historians. If the Saxon Wittenagemot is allowed to be a parliament, Derby, as a royal borough, must have had a voice; but we have no perfect list.

The burgesses frequently chose their representatives out of the Corporation, and allowed them, while on duty, six and eight pence a day; which would well support the stile of a gentleman. But matters are rather altered with time; a member would now *give* his constituents six and eight pence a day to let him represent them.

EDWARD I.

1294. 23. William de la Cornere, Randalph Makeneye.

1297.

Year. Parl.
1297. 26. William Bourne de Derby, Nicklos de Lorimer.
1299. 28. Nicklos de Lorimor, Gervase de Derby.
1301. 30. Gervase de Wilnye, Adam le Rede.
1304. 33. John de la Corne, Richard Cardoyl.
1305. 34. John de Chadesdon, Gervase de Wileyne.
1306. 35. Hugh Alibon, Peter la Chapman.

EDWARD II.

1307. 1. John Chaddesdon, Gervase de Wilney.
1310. 4. Henry Alwaston, Thomas de Stade.
1311. 5. Thomas del Sted, Henry Bindetton.
1312. 6. Geffry de Leycestre, Robert de Breydsale.
1313. 7. John Fitz John, Henry Lomb.
1314. 8. Adam le Rede, William de Aleby.
1314. 8. William de Aleby, Adam le Rede.
1318. 12. Simon de Chester, Richard Breddon.
1318. 12. Alexander de Holand, John de Weston.
1325. 19. Henry le Carpenter, John Fitz Richard.

1327.

OF DERBY. 93

Year. Parl.
EDWARD III.
1327. 1. John Fitz Gilbert, Ferhun Tutbury.
1328. 2. Simon de Chester, John Collings.
1328. 2. Thomas Tulaxbar, Geffry Snayth.
1328. 2. William Nottingham, John Weston.
1330. 4. Simon de Nottingham, John de Weston.
1330. 4. William Nottingham, Simon Chedel.
1333. 7. Hugh Allibon, John Gibbonson.
1334. 8. John Gibbonson, ——— ———.
1335. 9. Nickolas Langford, John Fitz Thomas.
1336. 9. Simon de Chester, John Gibbenson.
1337. 10. John Fitz Willyam, Thomas Tuttebury.
1338. 11. William de Derby, John Hache, Robert Allibon.
1338. 11. William de Derby, Robert de Weston.
1338. 11. Simon de Chester, Robert Allibon.
1338. 11. Henry del Howe, Robert Saundry.
1339. 12. Alexander Holland, John Weston.
1339. 12. John Gibbonson, Thomas Preston.
1339. 12. Thomas Titbury, Thomas Thurmondsley.
1341. 14. Thomas de Tutbury, Thomas Derby.

1341.

Year. Parl.

1341. 14. Richard de Trowell, Peter de Quarndon.
1342. 15. Simon de Nottingham, Thomas de Derby.
1344. 17. William de Nottingham, Simon de Chester.
1348. 21. William de Chaddesdon, Thomas de Tutbury.
1350. 23. William Gilbert, John de Chaddesdon.
1351. 24. Thomas Tutbury, William de Derby.
1354. 27. William Chester, Richard Chelford.
1355. 28. Thomas Tutbury, Henry Diddound.
1355. 28. Edmund Toucher, John Bech.
1356. 29. William Ennington, William Nayle.
1358. 31. William de Chester, William Nayle.
1361. 34. Peter Prentiz, William de Rossington.
1362. 35. Peter Prentiz, William de Rossington.
1363. 36. John Trowell, John Weeke.
1364. 37. John Bradon, Robert Allibon.
1365. 38. William Chestre, John Gilbert.
1366. 39. John Berd, William Sese.
1369. 42. John de Brakkeley, William Glasyere.

1370.

Year. Parl.
1370. 43. John Preest, John de Brakkelly.
1372. 45. John Trowell, ——— ———.
1373. 46. William Chestre, John Gilberd.
1374. 47. William Pakeman, Roger Allibon.
1377. 50. William Groos, John de Berdee.

RICHARD II.

1378. 2. John de Haye, Richard de Trowell.
1378. 2. Henry Flanstead, Roger Allibon.
1379. 3. Richard Dell, Roger Ashe.
1382. 6. Thomas Toppeleyse, John Haye.
1383. 7. William Pakeman, John Bowyer.
1383. 7. Richard de Trowell, John Gibbon.
1384. 8. Richard Sherman, John de Stockes.
1385. 9. Richard Trowell, John Dell.
1386. 10. John Stod, John Prentis.
1388. 12. William Pakeman, Hugh Adam.
1389. 13. John del Heye, John de Stokes.
1391. 15. Richard Sheteman, Thomas Dorking.
1394. 18. William Grosse, John de Stoke.
1396. 20. William Grosse, Thomas Shere.

HENRY IV.

1399. 1. John Stookes, Thomas Docking.
1402. 4. Elias del Stok. Richard de Trowell.
1404. 6. John del Stokes, John Prentiz.

1406.

Year. Parl.
1406. 8. Thomas Goldsmith, John Fairclogh.
1410. 12. John Brazier, Thomas Shore.

HENRY V.

1413. 1. Elias del Stock, ─────.
1414. 2. Elias del Stock, Thomas Rigway.
1415. 3. Elias del Stock, Roger Welley.
1417. 5. Robert Ireland, Thomas Steppingstone.
1419. 7. Thomas Goldsmith, John Fairclogh.
1420. 8. Robert Smith, Richard Browne.
1421. 9. Ralph Shore, John Spicer.

HENRY VI.

1422. 1. John Stokes, John Barkere.
1423. 2. John de Both, Elias Dell.
1424. 3. John Stokes, Elias Dell.
1425. 4. Roger Wolley, Henry Crabbe.
1427. 6. Nicholas Meysham, John de Stokkys.
1429. 8. John de Bathe, Elias Stokkys.
1430. 9. Thomas Stokkes, Robert Smith.
1432. 11. John Booth, Robert Sutton.
1434. 13. John Bothe, Thomas Stokeys.
1436. 15. Thomas Stokks, Elias Tildesley.
1441. 20. Thomas Stokkys, Henry Spicer.
1446. 25. Thomas Chatley, Robert Mundy.
1448. 27. Thomas Chatterley, John Spycer.

1449.

Year. Parl.
1449. 28. Richard Chitterley, Thomas Chitterley.
1450. 29. Thomas Acard, Thomas Bradshawe.
1454. 33. John Bird, Edward Lovel.
1459. 38. John Bird, William Hunter.

EDWARD IV.
1468. 7. Thomas Bakynton, Thomas Allestre.
1473. 12. John Newton, Roger Wilkinson.
1478. 17. John Briddle, John Newton.

HENRY VIII.
1542. 33. Thomas Sutton, William Alestre.

EDWARD VI.
1553. 6. Robert Ragge, William Alestry.

MARY.
1553. 1. George Sutton, George Charney.
1553. 1. William Alestry, George Stringer.
1553. 1. William Moor, Richard Baynbrygge.
1554. 2. William Moor, Richard Baynbrygge.
1554. 2. Richard Warde, William Alestry.
1555. 3. Richard Warde, William Alestry.
1556. 4. James Thacker, William Baynbrigge.
1559. 5. James Thacker, William Baynbrigge.

ELIZABETH.
1563. 5. William Moor, William Baynbrigge.

1571.

98   THE HISTORY

Year. Parl.
1571. 13. Robert Stringer, Robert Baynbrigge.
1572. 14. Robert Stringer, Tristram Tirwhite.
1585. 27. Henry Beaumont, William Botham.
1586. 28. WilliamBotham,RobertBaynbrigge.
1589. 31. William Botham, Richard Fletcher.
1593. 35. William Botham, Robert Stringer.
1601. 43. Peter Ewer, John Baxter.

JAMES I.

1603. 1. John Baxter, Edmund Slighe.
1620. 18. Timothy Leving, Edward Leech.
1623. 21. Edward Leech, Timothy Leving.

CHARLES I.

1625. 1. Edward Leech, Timothy Leving.
1625. 1. Sir Henry Crofts, John Thorogood.
1627. 3. Peter Mainwaring, Timothy Leving.
1639. 15. William Alestry, Nathaniel Hallowes.
1640. 16. William Alestry, Nathaniel Hallowes.

COMMONWEALTH.

Gervase Bennet, John Dalton.

CHARLES II.

1660. 11. John Dalton, Roger Alestry.
1662. 13. Roger Alestry, John Dalton.
1679. 30. George Vernon, Anchetil Gray.
1681. 32. Anchetil Gray, George Vernon.

JAMES

Year. Parl.
JAMES II.
1685.　1. John Coke, William Alestry.

WILLIAM III.
1689.　1. Anchetil Gray, John Coke.
1690.　2. Anchetil Gray, Robert Wilmot.
1695.　7. Lord Henry Cavendish, John Bagnold.
1698. 10. Lord Henry Cavendish, George Vernon.
1700. 12. James Cavendish, Sir Charles Pye.
1701. 13. John Harpur, Lord James Cavendish.

ANNE.
1702.　1. John Harpur, Thomas Stanhope.
1705.　4. Lord James Cavendish, Thomas Parker.
1707.　6. Lord James Cavendish, Sir Thomas Parker.
1710.　9. Sir Richard Leving, John Harpur.
1713. 12. Nathaniel Curzon, Edward Mundy.

GEORGE I.
1714.　1. Lord James Cavendish, William Stanhope.
1722.　8. Lord James Cavendish, William Bayly.

Year. Parl.

GEORGE II.

1727. 1. Lord James Cavendish, William Stanhope.
1734. 7. Lord James Cavendish, Charles Stanhope.
1741. 14. Lord James Cavendish, John Stanhope.
          Lord James resigned the following year, and Lord Duncannon chosen.
1747. 20. Lord Duncannon, John Stanhope.
1754. 27. Lord Frederick Cavendish, George Venables Vernon.

GEORGE III.

1761. 2. Lord Frederick Cavendish, George Venables Vernon.
1768. 9. Lord Frederick Cavendish, William Fitzherbert.
1774. 15. Lord Frederick Cavendish, Daniel Parker Coke.
1780. 21. Lord George Henry Augustus Cavendish, Edward Coke.
1784. 25. Lord George Henry Augustus Cavendish, Edward Coke.
1790. 30. Lord George Henry Augustus Cavendish, Edward Coke.
          1796.

Year. Parl.
1796. 36. Lord George Henry Augustus Cavendish, Edward Coke.
1797. 37. Hon. George Walpole, son of Lord Walpole, *vice* Cavendish.
1800. 40. Edward Coke, Hon. George Walpole.
1801. 41. Edward Coke, Hon. George Walpole.
1806. 46. Edward Coke, William Cavendish, eldest son of Lord George Cavendish.
1807. 47. Edward Coke, William Cavendish.
1812. 52. Edward Coke, Henry Frederick Compton Cavendish; another son of Lord George Cavendish.

It is curious in these lists, which continue about 500 years, to observe the rude state of letters. There seems to have been no fixed principles in the use of the alphabet, for a man seldom spelt his name twice alike; nor is it a wonder we see confusion, for very few could handle the pen. A gradual improvement may easily be traced. We also observe the fluctuation of parliaments; sometimes three or four in a year, and sometimes thirteen or fourteen years without.

The

The choice of representatives is with the freemen: the Mayor is the returning officer.

The number of burgesses may be estimated by the contested elections. Perhaps they are about 900. In that of 1700, between Sir Charles Pye and Sir John Harpur, great-grand-father to the present Baronet, the number of voters were 537; but as Pye was foremost by 137, the contest was given up. In another in 1742, between Lord Duncannon and German Pole, there were 646; but the latter, being 46 behind, relinquished. Thomas Rivett and Thomas Stanhope, in 1748, produced 643. But the most violent contest upon record was in 1714, between Nathaniel Curzon, father to the present Lord Scarsdale, and Edward Mundy on one side; and Lord James Cavendish and Sir William Stanhope, on the other: the opposition rose to such violence, that even the highways, hedges, and sinks of obscurity, were ransacked for electors. The number polled was 862.

The

The Devonshire interest in the choice of representatives is very considerable; the amiable character of the family, and their repeated acts of kindness, have justly endeared them to the inhabitants.

FAIRS.

From the renewal of charters, Derby enjoys seven Fairs : January 25 ; March 25 ; Friday in Easter-Week; first Friday in May; Friday in Whitson-Week ; July 25 (St. James); and September 29.

The market-day is on Friday.

The following gentlemen of Derby have served the office of Sheriff for the county:

1616. John Bullock.
1673. Sir Simon Degge.
1719. Samuel Burton.
1742. John Gisborn.
1744. William Roberts.
1757. Thomas Rivett.
1760. Thomas Bainbrigge.
1768. Samuel Crompton.
1790. Thomas Macklin Wilson.

COURT OF REQUESTS.

While we adhere to that excellent maxim, adopted by all civilized nations, *That every man ought to have his right*, a Court of Conscience will be found necessary. So long as it shall be deemed prudent to put a period to quarrels among neighbours, so long will a Court of Conscience be useful. The privilege of going to law is the birthright of an Englishman; lop off this fruitful branch of British freedom, and the tree of liberty will be left naked. As the expences of the court are exceedingly small, he enjoys his birthright at an easy price.

This Court was erected in Derby in 1766; is held in the Guildhall every third Tuesday: about *one hundred* of the inhabitants are commissioners, that is, the principal part of the town; a number perfectly sufficient to dam up the stream of business. Three constitute a bench. Mr. Harrison

is

is clerk. About thirty causes appear every court day.

ECCLESIASTICAL HISTORY.

There is no feature in the human mind which marks the character of a people more than their religious cast. Liberality of sentiment produces gentleness of conduct; while a strenuous faith leads towards ferocity: the moment a man becomes opinionated, all arguments are lost; reason and bigotry never associate: if he no longer examines, he can no longer judge; his own stamp alone is genuine, he utters it in currency, and prohibits all others.

The History of the English Church, during the last seventeen hundred years, may be comprized in fewer words than would fill a folio. The Romans found the Britons, what the Britons found them, *Pagans*. Their disputes did not so much regard religon as dominion. From the third to the sixth century, Christianity crept

crept into this island with mild and cautious steps; and met, in its progress, many a cruel butcher. From its establishment to the ninth century, the professors, having none to destroy them, destroyed one another. Murder was the consequence of a difference of opinion in doctrinal points; and hundreds of lives were lost because they could not agree whether Easter-Sunday should be this week or the next. Matters being settled in blood, the Church may be fairly said to have been in a trance, till the reign of Henry the Eighth; during which time the Pontiff exercised an absolute dominion, unknown in the history of man; even Christian *Princes* were only gilded slaves: body, soul, conscience, and property, were offered at the papal throne. But, waking from her slumbers, in the morning of letters, a dreadful contest ensued between Papist and Protestant; and the church was weakly supported by one of the most powerful elements in nature, *fire*. Victory, in the reign of Elizabeth, declared for the Protestants, and
Hierarchy

Hierarchy erected her strong holds upon the ruin of the enemy.—The love of power is nearly equal to the love of life: the Church and the Crown entered into partnership, and ruled the people with an iron hand. The note of the day was *prerogative*. Nature recoils at oppression: if we tread even upon a worm, the feeble animal will return, as if to revenge its cause. The injured nation in 1642, after groaning forty years, threw off the yoke, when the *people of God* stepped forward, and over-turned the kingdom. Thus power, and the abuse of power, are synonymous terms.—These violent church-rulers gave way, in their turn, to a superior force in the beginning of Charles the Second; when the Hierarchy again, like a bed of mushrooms, recovered itself in a day, and bound the antagonist; over whom it yet holds the rod; but the gentle spirit of the times forbids the use: and now the taste of the day is mitres, crosiers, robes, rochets, and glebe-lands.—Opinions never hurt a church; but can our pride appear more ridiculous than when we force ours upon others, or prohibit a man's own? This anxious solicitude to make converts has been the bane of the Christian world.

The great number of churches yet in being, and of religious houses which are gone to ruin, indicate that Derby was strongly tinctured with religious fervour. But the benign plant of ecclesiastical liberty never flourished here, except it has taken root within these fifty years.

From the solicitation of the inhabitants, Richard the First granted, by charter, to them and their heirs, the power of expelling every Jew who then resided in, or ever after should approach, Derby. This is the first ecclesiastical anecdote mentioned in history; and I am sorry it is not more to the honour of my native place. I trust, however, for the sake of humanity, they have long ago burnt the charter. If a Jew, or a Christian, break the laws of equity by injuring another, those laws ought to punish him, by forcing reparation; otherwise, he ought to be free of society. His religion and his abode

abode are objects of his own choice. Here we first observe that intolerant spirit which, for 500 years, haunted Derby. Ill neighbourhood, animosity, and persecution, were the result. Why this evil spirit was not laid in the *Red*-sea, or in any other sea, is best known to the Clergy.

The man who *has* power, may oblige him who has none to *act* like him; but he cannot oblige him to *think* like him. Thought is free; action should follow thought. No man can be free, except his actions are his own; and while no injury arises from them, no power ought to controul them: hence appears the absurdity of punishing for religious conduct. Religion is allowed by all parties to be composed of *meekness* and *love;* but in all ages it has been supported by a spirit of blustering. *That* has ever been the *truest* which was the strongest. Power is the criterion of right. A powerful church is a powerful oppressor; and becomes a powerful state engine. No system can stand examination but that of perfect freedom; for, should
the

the least infringement be allowed, the system falls. If a man's faith and practice be ever so absurd, they are his own; they are private property; to which he has the same right as to the coat he wears, or the air he breathes; for should a second person deprive him of these, because they are infamous, a third, for the same reason, may deprive the second; here then the fabric moulders, and it cannot be erected upon another basis. The Scriptures, as a rule of rectitude, never taught one man to take that which is the property of another. Errors in belief arise from the weakness of judgement: if we err in plain cases, it is no wonder we err in the mysterious. This weakness, being no fault, cannot merit punishment.—In a recent conversation with my friend *Moses Solomon*, if a Jew can be the friend of a Christian, he delivered, what some would deem an absurd belief, " That the Rabbies of their church had still the power of working miracles; a power which must be attended with other powers equally great. That Constantinople contained 600,000 Jewish

Jewish families! Amsterdam nearly as many! That the generations of men dwindled in size every age; and in time would be reduced to pigmies. That in the days of David they were ten yards high; and that Absalom, being a fine young fellow, was considerably taller. In those of Moses, they were twenty; but that Adam was so tall as to prevent the sun-beams from reaching the earth over his head. That Christ was an impostor, and had done irreparable mischief to that religion which he ought to have confirmed. That Dr. Priestley was culpable in attempting to convert the Israelites; and that he would never succeed:" which perhaps was the truest sentence he uttered. I assured him that, however his sentiments differed from those of others, yet, as none were injured by them, none could claim a power over them; and that, instead of being repelled, he ought to be supported.—Amazed, says the pious reader, Would you allow such monstrous tenets? Yes.—Perhaps you would suffer the Heathen to worship the Sun? Certainly:

Certainly: he worships the Saviour of the world; so do you.—And would you suffer the Mahometan absurdities to pass? I would: nay, I go farther; I would support that religion whose former practice I am going to condemn.

In 1556, when the faggot was the barrier between truth and falsehood, a religious and harmless girl, of All Saints' parish, named Joan Waste, who was born blind, and assisted her father, a rope-maker, in his calling, was accused, by some officious neighbours, before that ignorant Doctor, Ralph Barns, bishop of Lichfield and Coventry, of denying the real presence in the Sacrament. The bigot attempted to persuade her into his faith; upon which terms he offered to secure her salvation. But not being able to convert her to *his* religion, he was determined to put a stop to her own, therefore condemned her to the flames, and consigned her to the bailiffs of Derby for execution.

This innocent victim to cruelty, aged 22, was, August 1, led to All Saints, like a criminal,

criminal, preparatory to her suffering; and from the church conducted, in solemn procession, to Windmill-pit, near the Turnpike, upon the Burton-road, about a mile from the church; in the centre of which she suffered the torture of fire with humble fortitude. It is matter of the utmost surprize, that the innocence of her life, her youth, her sex, and her misfortune, did not operate with her severe judges. Impressed with her melancholy fate, even in early childhood, I have examined the spot where she suffered; and, by the help of an infant imagination, *believed* I discovered the relics of the burnt faggots; which, like a random faith, founded in weakness, could be no more than the powerful operations of fancy.

Those people who are not employed in some active pursuit, have time to dabble into the concerns of others—a sure indication of quarrels. This being the case at Derby, perpetual differences ensued between Papist and Protestant under the Tudors; and between Whig and Tory under the Stuarts. The town was rent in the reigns of Queen Anne and George the First in favour of the Church, though no enemy was near it. There was only one small congregation of Dissenters, who were obliged to keep a nocturnal watch to preserve their meeting-house from dissection; but not a Roman Catholic, an Independent, Baptist, Israelite, or even a harmless Quaker, could be found in the place. This irksome piece of disjointed neighbourhood was increased by that incendiary, Dr. Sacheverell, whom the Sheriff, George Sacheverell, of Callow, his cousin, admitted into the pulpit of All Saints, in 1709, to preach the Assize Sermon. He fed the people with food to their taste; such as himself had received from the disappointed Atterbury: he told the world, "The Church was in danger;" and he told them true; for he had set it in a flame. Had *Butler* written his Hudibras thirty years later, I should have supposed he had had Sacheverell in his eye when he talked of his *Drum Ecclesiastick*.

CHURCHES.

South East View of St. Almonds Church.

CHURCHES.

We are told, that at the Conquest there were six churches in Derby: two belonged to the King; one to Ferrers, afterwards Earl of Derby; another to Alselin; a fifth to Ralph de Norman; and the last to Edric. The present five, no doubt, are part of the number; and the sixth must have been St. Mary's, because no other will answer the description.

The stately All Saints, attended by four diminutive churches, viewed at a distance, brings to the mind a hen and chickens: but if the simile should be thought too grovelling, we can present one more elevated, in the moon attended by four little stars.

ST. ALKMUND'S

Stands at the North end of the town. It was probably erected in the eighth century. Alcred was crowned King of Northumberland

thumberland in 765; but was deposed by
a faction, in favour of Ethelred, after a
reign of nine years. His son, Alkmund,
headed a party to reinstate his father; but,
being unsuccessful, was put to death in
800, by Ardulph, the reigning prince.
Misfortunes create the saint; canonization
follows; and one small step farther brings
us to miracles; thus Alkmund became a
saint and a martyr. He was first interred
at Lettleshull, in Shropshire; but that place
being thought too mean for a worker of
miracles, he was removed to Derby, and
deposited in St. Alkmund's; whence the
name. He had many devotees at his shrine;
but not so many as Becket, though as expert at miracles.

The Church, in early times, was given
to the abbey of Derley; and continued till
the Dissolution, when Henry seized it;
and it rested in the Crown till his daughter, Queen Mary, gave it to the Corporation of Derby, who have the presentation.
It is a vicarage, value £.11. 6s. 8d. in the
King's books; which must have been a
mistake,

mistake, or some of the emoluments were lost; for in the reign of George the First the income was only eight pounds *per ann.* and divine service was performed but once a quarter.—An old batchelor of the name of Goodwin, of an ancient family in Derby, possessed an estate of £.60 a year. How will you dispose of your fortune? says Mr. Cantril, minister of St. Alkmund's. " I am at a loss," replied Goodwin, " for I have no near relations." Here was a fine opening for Cantril to increase his income, and for Goodwin to save his soul, by giving that property to pious uses which he could keep no longer. Eloquence is seldom wanting to promote our interest. " My church," says the parson, " stands desolate; instead of being a place of regular worship, it is only a nursery for owls and bats. No act of charity can surpass that of promoting religion." " Then I will give £.10 *per annum* to St. Alkmund's at my death," says Goodwin; " and the residue at the death of my nephew :" which last happened about the year 1734.

The

The steeple contains six musical bells. The parish extends as far as Chester, Little-Eaton, Derley, and Quarndon. Income about £.100 *per annum*. Vicar, the Rev. Thomas Manlove.

ST. MICHAEL'S

Stands near the last; and, like that, was a member of Derley, was seized by Henry, and given by Mary to the Corporation; is a vicarage, with the small revenue of £.4. 11s. 11d. in the King's books. It is united with St. Warburgh's, and has service once a month. Every thing is upon a small scale, as if our pious ancestors were determined to build a church, but were barely able; the church-yard is little, the church less, and in the steeple are three small bells.

The village of Alveston belongs to this parish. Great disputes arising between the inhabitants of this hamlet, and the vicar of St. Michael's, concerning tithes, it was formally agreed, in 1499, by the Bishop of

G. Montgomery Delin.   B. Jamock sculp.

South West View of St. Michaels Church.

South West View of St. Werburgh's Church.

of the diocese, the Abbot and Convent of Derley, and the Vicar, on one side; and the people of Alveston, on the other; that the latter should pay the Vicar three pounds *per annum* for ever in lieu of tithes.—A losing agreement for the parsonage; but a bargain worth quarreling for by the inhabitants. It was farther stipulated in the above agreement, that they should regularly attend divine service at St. Michael's; a practice long forgotten. Another superannuated article was, that they should, upon no account, sickness excepted, omit attendance at the feast of the *Relics.*

ST. WARBURGH'S.

Is situated on the West side of Derby upon Markeaton-brook. Probably this was one of the churches vested in the Crown at the Conquest, and there continued till King Stephen granted it to Derley-abbey. At the Dissolution it was recovered back, and is now in the hands of the Sovereign. The income was valued at £.39. 11s. This advanced

vanced stipend was owing to a chantry in the church, well endowed, which is annexed to the income.

This church and steeple were lovingly united together, according to the canonical points of the compass, the church to the East, and its companion towards the West; but, in 1601, a flood upon Markeaton-brook sapping the foundation, the steeple fell. To gain firmer ground, they erected it on the East side of the church, contrary to the situation of steeples; and November 5, 1698, the church fell, owing to another flood, which produced a paltry rhime from John Pegge,

Fifth of November, Gun-powder Plot,
The Church is fall'n; and why not?

This wicked distich, without measure, harmony, or thought (for John was never able to think), which ought to have been treated with a smile, raised the clamour of the Establishment against the Dissenters, for John was one of that body. The steeple has five bells. Osmaston is part of the parish. The income, united with St. Michael's, is

about

South East View of St. Peters Church

about £.150; and the Rev. Charles Hope is vicar of both.

ST. PETER'S.

This is in the South, and probably the other church belonging to the Crown at the Conquest. This, as well as St. Warburgh's, was given to Derley-abbey in the reign of King Stephen. Robert Liversage, a dyer, of Derby, founded a chapel in this church in 1530, and ordered divine service to be celebrated every Friday; in which were to attend thirteen people, of either sex, each to be rewarded with a silver penny; as much *then* as would have supported a frugal person. The porches, like those of Bethesda, were crowded with people, who waited for the moving of the doors, as the others for that of the waters. While the spiritual serjeant beat up for volunteers at a penny advance, recruits would never be wanting. A sufficient congregation was not doubted; nor their quarreling for the money. The priest found his hearers in
that

that disorder which his prayers could not rectify: they frequently fought; but not the good fight of faith; nor did ill-neighbourhood end with Friday. The hearer used to pay the preacher; but here the case was reversed. We learn that no scheme is so likely to fill a church as the silver penny; that good silver will *draw* more than good sermons; that no devotion is valid that is bought with a price; and that a penny will make a hypocrite.

In the same church was a chantry to St. Mary; but, as no premium was given for attendance, perhaps the priest sung to the walls.

St. Peter's fell in the common ruin, and was vested in the Crown till Queen Mary granted it to the Corporation. As the profits of the chapel and the chantry were united with the benefice, the income was augmented to £.37. 15s. It is a vicarage. The steeple, a musical instrument, is tuned with six bells. The villages of Normanton, Bolton, and Litchurch, are members of this parish.

The

South View of All Saints Church

The riches accumulated by Derley Abbey were amazing. The violent piety of those dark times heaped upon it a continual increase of power, prodigious wealth, and a great part of the adjacent lands: it carried with it all the churches in Derby, except All Saints. But, at the Dissolution, they not only again rested upon their former basis, but their stipends, being found insufficient for their support, drew after them several members of the abbey, which are the villages appropriated to each church.

The presentation is in the family of Dixey; the annual value £.130.; and the Rev. Richard Ward is the Vicar.

ALL SAINTS.

The stranger, who wanders through Derby in quest of objects worthy of remark, will find some defects, and more beauties: but when he arrives at All Saints, he arrives at the chief excellence — the pride of the place. It stands as a prince among subjects; a giant among dwarfs.
Viewed

Viewed at any distance, or in any attitude, the associated ideas of taste, grandeur, and beauty, fascinate the mind; the eye is captivated, and continually returns to its object, but never tires. Some pride, more sense, and still more judgement, must have combined in our forefathers in the construction of this noble tower: they wrought, and we enjoy the credit of their labour.

A church in Derby, where the stone is not of a loose texture, will endure much more than a thousand years. As time has worn out one church and one steeple, we may fairly suppose this was erected early in the Saxon government; is the oldest in Derby; the only one known to have been rebuilt, Warburgh's excepted; nor should I much doubt, as this spot is the most inviting, but the Britons had here a temple.

Its name, *All Saints*, is modern; in old writings it is *Allhallows;* and it is yet so called by the lower class, who rarely change their mode of speech: the two names, however, mean the same thing.

But

But it is doubtful whether even *Allhallows* is the original name; there is some reason to suppose it was *St. Mary's;* how else can we account for the name of a principal street leading towards it, *St. Mary-gate?* This could not be derived from the chapel at St. Mary's Bridge, because that stands at the verge, and the other in the centre, of the town. But this being the principal church, and St. Mary the principal saint, might reasonably go together. In after-ages, the people chose to place Mary at the bridge, and honour the great church with *all the Saints* that ever the Pope dispatched to heaven; besides, there is mentioned a St. Leonard, whose habitation is no where found: perhaps he lodged at the chapel on the bridge prior to Mary.

This church, in the reign of Edward the First, was free from all ecclesiastical jurisdiction, that of the Pope excepted. It is still free; it was besides collegiate; had a governor, who was dean of Lincoln; and seven collegians, who probably resided in the house, now the residence of Daniel Parker

Parker Coke, Esq. North of the Church, which yet bears the name of *The College*. They possessed lands, tithes, and other emoluments, to the amount of more than £.600. a year of our present money. All this fell into the rapacious hands of Henry the Eighth; but Queen Mary, in the first of her reign, granted the church and part of the property to the Corporation, in whose gift it now is, and is a curacy.

The steeple, in a decayed state, was taken down in the reign of Henry the Eighth, and the present elegant piece of architecture set in its place. Upon a fillet, on the North, in old English, easily read, is *Young Men and Maids*. Tradition tells us, that the steeple was erected to the height of that inscription by the voluntary contributions of the youth of both sexes; a generous benefaction, which indicates they were strangers to poverty, irreligion, and covetousness. On the South side is another inscription, *not* easily read. This beautiful Gothic building is 178 feet high; the most superb in that part of the kingdom. I am told there is but

but one higher in England, Boston. I saw a dog fall from the top, and was surprized at the length of time he took in his descent, owing to his beating the air in his struggles to rise. Ten bells, and a set of chimes, grace the internal part.

While the steeple was down, the church stood solitary, having lost her helpmate; but in 1722 the church was taken away, and the steeple stood silent, as if lamenting the loss of his. A few of the ancient monuments were reserved and replaced; but the generations which had accumulated for ages in this repository of the dead, fell a prey to the pick-axe. The last intelligence of the old inhabitants was lost for ever. Monuments may preserve the dead; but what can preserve monuments! The fine hand of the artist holds up for a while the history of the defunct; but the rough hand of the labourer, or, at least that of indefatigable time, destroys his work. Upon one of the galleries in gold letters was written, " This gallery was erected in 16 .., by —— Sutton, Esq. of King's-mead, near Derby."

Derby." Two remarks arise from this intelligence: that *King's-mead,* not Nuns-green, was the original name; and that the habitation, once sufficiently grand for an Esquire, would now disgrace the pride even of a shoe-maker. His house is yet standing, marked with an elevated white porch projecting from the front.

The design of the present church was done by Gibbs, for which he received £25. The curate, Dr. Hutchinson, not only subscribed £40. but, being a man of genteel address, charged himself with raising the whole money, and executing a masterly work, without a shilling expence to his parish. He was a complete master of the art of begging. The people to whom he applied were not able to keep their money; it passed from their pockets to his own, as if by magic. Wherever he could recollect a person likely to contribute to this desirable work, he made no scruple to visit him at his own expence. He took a journey to London, to solicit the benefaction of Thomas Chambers, Esq. ancestor

of

of the Earl of Exeter, who gave him one hundred pounds. If a stranger passed through Derby, the Doctor's bow and his rhetoric were employed in the service of the church. His anxiety was urgent; and his powers so prevailing, that he seldom failed of success. When the Waites fiddled at his door for a Christmas-box, instead of sending them away with a solitary shilling, he invited them in, treated them with a tankard of ale, and persuaded them out of a guinea. I have seen his list of subscribers, which are 589; and the sum £.3249. 11s. 6d. But it appears he could procure a man's *name* by his eloquence easier than his money; for 52 of the subscribers never paid their sums, amounting to £.137. 16s. 6d. The remaining £.3111. 15s. being defective, he procured a brief, which added £.598. 5s. 6d. more. Still, though assiduity was not wanting, money was; he therefore sold six burying places in the vault for six guineas; and twelve of the principal seats in the church, by inch of candle, for

K   £.475.

£.475. 13s. which were purchased as freeholds by the first inhabitants.

Pride influences our actions; nor will it bear contradiction. As the Doctor raised the money, he justly expected to have the disposal; but the parish considered themselves neglected, and repeatedly thwarted his measures, till, provoked by reiterated insults, he threw up the management, and left them in a labyrinth of their own creating. The result was, a considerable expence upon themselves. Some things he intended, were never finished; and some never begun. He preached the first sermon, November 25, 1725, from David, *I was glad when they said unto me, let us go into the house of the Lord.*

This modern pile is divided into two unequal parts by a range of iron palisades, fabricated by Bakewell, at the expence, as an artist informed me, of £.500; but the account says only £.181. The West, which is the largest, is appropriated for public worship, with a beautiful gallery and organ. The East side of this elegant
iron

iron work is separated into three parts; one for chusing the mayor, and other vestry business; the centre is the chancel; and the third, the dormitory of the Devonshire family. Here lie the worthies of liberty, who possessed the illustrious name of Cavendish. Here, at full length, is seen the monument of the Countess of Shrewsbury, constructed under her own inspection, in the dress of her day. She purchased this last seat of the family from the Corporation, into which 29 of the dead have found their way. She saw the end of four husbands, procured a dowry from each, was immensely rich, performed many works of charity and magnificence, continued a widow seventeen years, and died in 1607, in extreme age.

The noted Richard Croshaw, with his nail-hammer and leathern doublet, has also a monument. He, like some others of his townsmen, seeing only poverty in the prospect before him, went to London to shun it. Talents, and a field to improve them, furnished him with a fortune of £.10,000. Others, he justly supposed, might feel, in his native place, that distress which he had felt himself, therefore he left £.4,000. to the Corporation for charities; and there is not a pauper in the borough, who is a stranger to *Croshaw's dole*. The infant mouth, unable to feed itself, which has been fed by his bounty, may live to return a tribute of gratitude to its benefactor. He left £.20. *per annum* for a lecture every Friday. He died in 1631. This amiable character is said to have staid in London during a plague, to administer comfort to distress, and escaped the contagion.—The next monument to this belongs to a person of the name of Wheeler, who quitted London to shun that dreadful calamity in 1665; but died at Derby the following year: though he travelled far, he could not travel out of the reach of death.

Another monument mentions the age and death of ——— Carter in 1696.

A stone is preserved in the vestry, the date 1400, which records the memory of John Law, sub-dean of All Saints; his

figure

figure in scroll lines, as big as life, is in high preservation. I think these are all the monuments that survived the wreck of the old church.

An elegant monument was erected in 1737 by the Countess of Exeter, to the memory of her parents, Thomas Chambers and his lady.

Many charities appertain to this church, the bequests of the pious, but ill-judging, Christian; for we had better support the living, by the living, than by the dead.

Ward's dole, left in 1673, was then six four-penny loaves a week; now increased to £.21. *per ann.*

Isabella Moore left the same year £.5. *per ann.* for putting out apprentices; now increased to £.17.

William Duffield left £.2. *per ann.* to buy gowns for poor widows; now £.8. *per ann.*

Rev. Joseph Smetman left in 1652 twenty-six shillings for sixteen widows of All Saints, and ten for those of St. Alkmund's.

Alice

Alice Beaumont left thirty shillings a year to be laid out in groat loaves for widows. This issues out of a house near the top of Full-Street, occupied in my day by ——— Peach, an attorney.

Elizabeth Stone left ten shillings to be paid every Easter Sunday to widows of the Establishment.

Joice Harpur gave £.10. towards building a workhouse; and ten shillings a year to the poor for ever.

Exclusive of these small charities, which perhaps originated in pride, to perpetuate a name, there are thirteen others of the annual value, when left, of twenty-nine pounds eight shillings, which are lost for want of attention. Perhaps they would now have brought one hundred and fifty pounds. Here then is a fatal instance of mistaken charity. Every bequest becomes a multiplied temptatation. Few legacies pass entire through many generations. While the trust sleeps, the tenant becomes a landlord; or while charity sleeps, the trust pockets a field.

After

After this work was committed to the press, an abstract of Queen Mary's grant to the Corporation, of a few scattered fragments belonging to Derley Abbey, fell into my hands. These consisted of fifty-seven separate estates.

It appears, that in consideration of two hundred and sixty-six pounds, thirteen shillings, and four pence, paid by the Corporate Body into the hands of the Queen's *beloved Counsellor Edward Parkhorn*, that she assigned to them the above property, about 86 houses, chiefly in Derby, with about 216 acres of land, in and near the town; all the mills in the manor; four of these were upon the Derwent; and three of them fulling mills. To this ample gift, which was property arising from the blind zeal of the dying, and was viewed with regret by the heirs who were living, the Queen added the donation of *Heath*, in the county of Derby, with its manorial rights. This alone was a clear annual income of £77. 2s. 7d. The united value of these bequests, I apprehend,

prehend, was about £280. a year; now worth more than £2000.

Out of the issues of *Heath* the Corporation were to pay, every Michaelmas, £41. 15s. 10d. into the exchequer; and out of the fifty-seven estates one shilling *per ann.* to Thomas Ward, and his heirs; ten pence to the chamberlains; one shilling to the church-wardens; and thirteen pounds, six shillings, and eight pence, to two priests, for performing duty in All Saints; six pounds, thirteen shillings, and four pence, to the minister of St. Alkmund's; and one pound, thirteen shillings, and four-pence, to the bailiff, to defray the expence of collecting the rents. The grant also ordered a free-school to be erected, and thirteen pounds, six shillings, and eight-pence, for the support of a master and usher.

Perhaps it would be difficult for the most penetrating eye to find out the fifty-seven estates: like the guineas of a Rake, their number has long been wasting. What trust can withstand fifty-seven temptations!

The

The author of the abstract farther remarks, and with bitterness of soul, 84 different charities left by private persons to the several parishes, and chiefly entrusted to the Corporation as guardians. Many of these also, like the guineas above, are vanished, and no traces left. Before a dying man disposes of that which belongs to his rightful successor, he may consider whether he can deposit it in the hands of a perpetual trust, who will not want it themselves? and, who will not slumber when *a tenant wants it?* and whether, instead of making a saint of himself, he is not making a knave of another?

Were an officer of each parish selected, and empanelled into a jury of five, to try the probity of past ages, they would either open scenes of misconduct, or they would find in their verdict for All Saints,

19 benefactions of the original value of - - - £66 11 4 *per ann.*
14 belonging to St. Michael's, - -. ⸺ 11 14 11

St.

		per ann.	
St. Peter's 14,	£.61	1	6
23 appropriated to St. Werburg's,	73	12	7
And 14 to St. Alkmund's	19	8	6

There is also a piece of ground of ten or twelve acres, between Nunsgreen and the Derwent, called The Lamp Close, bequeathed ages back, for the support of the lamps; but whether it still preserves its *use*, or only its *name*, I am unable to say.

The western boundary of All Saints church-yard ought to have formed a line with the houses in Iron-gate and Kingstreet; the trespass, which is of little use, injures the road, and hurts the eye.——— While in solemn thought I range over these gloomy regions of the dead, and peruse the names I have long known, among the vast number of *Here lies*, I reflect with sorrow that here lies the dust of my family; characters of still life, who lived their day and retired.

The emoluments arising to the curate, who is presented by the Corporation, are about £130. *per ann.* .

DISSENTERS.

DISSENTERS.

The people of Derby, strenuous for the Church, would not allow, half a century ago, even one Dissenting meeting-house; but their more moderate successors peaceably behold three, a Presbyterian, Independant, and Methodist. Perhaps there is not an *im*moderate Episcopalian in the place; or I could ask, if the Catholic, the Quaker, the Jew, and the Baptist, entered, wherein would the Church or the town suffer? Habits of communication dissipate prejudice, and reconcile us to each other.

MEETING IN FRIAR-GATE.

The Presbyterians, under the name of Puritans, had their private places of assembling in the days of Queen Elizabeth, James, and Charles; but those places were small, and are now unknown. Under the Oliverian power, the national religion

gion hit their sentiments, and they attended the churches. The Bartholomew Act, in 1662, discharged them; and they assembled, in various places, hidden from the magistrate. The bishop at length licensed St. Mary's chapel at the foot of the bridge; but this did not continue. They housed, in the reign of James the Second, in the wide yard, on the East side of Irongate, which communicated with the market-place, where they continued till the erection of the present meeting-house in Friar-gate; where, out of gratitude to King William, for giving them that liberty which they had a right to demand, they placed his arms over the pulpit. The present ministers are the Rev. James Pilkington and the Rev. ―― Philips.

THE METHODISTS

Erected a meeting-house in St. Michael's-lane, under that great divine, *John Wesley;* who, differing in sentiment from the sons of the Church, covets
not

North East View of the Calvinist Meeting House

not wealth, though all he possesses is not of more consequence than the small dust of the balance; but he covets more religion, though already possessed of more than half the Bench of Bishops.

INDEPENDANTS.

From a difference of judgement in religious points, which will ever happen among men, a separation took place in the congregation in Friar-gate, and the seceders erected a chapel for themselves by the brook in 1785. The Rev. John Smith, pastor.

RELIGIOUS HOUSES.

We have examined what we may fairly call the *living* places of worship; we now descend among the dead: but our information is as dark as their regions. *Dugdale* and *Tanner*, the principal authors upon whom we rely, are short and confused: their knowledge, united with tradition,

dition, and the topographical researches of a native, will barely compose a plausible tale. However they may vary in the number of these houses at Derby, there certainly were five: they mention six; an abbey of the order of St. Augustin; a nunnery of St. Benedict; another abbey of Dominicans; a cell of Cluniacs; and two houses for leprous persons, exclusive of St. Mary's church. None of these were mitred, or made a figure in the history of the times; neither are there the least traces of any of the buildings, except a small part of St. Mary's: two hundred and fifty years having destroyed all but their names. Though gone to decay, they were not so ancient as the churches. The principal of these houses was that of

ST. HELEN,

Of the order of St. Augustin, situated on the North side of Derby, supposed to have stood on the spot now a malt-house, behind the Plough, at the top of the walk. A
porter's

porter's lodge belonging to this house, in the angle, between the roads to Nunsgreen and Keddleston, now a fruit-house, probably gave the name to *Lodge-lane.*

Robert de Ferrers, the second Earl of Derby, in the reign of King Stephen, erected it; and, being devout and rich, amply endowed this holy retreat. But although it continued for ages, it did not flourish; for the pride of rivalship taking possession of the heart of Hugh the priest, who was dean of Derby, induced him, about thirty years after, to offer Albin, abbot of St. Helen's, all his lands in Derby and Derley, with the patronage of St. Peter's, if he would erect an abbey in Derley, still in the same parish, but a mile to the North. Albin joyfully accepted a proposition which would gratify his pride, raise his revenue, enable him to quit the smoke of Derby, and keep his Lent upon the delightful banks of the Derwent. From this time St. Helen's dwindled; and Derley, from astonishing bequests, flourished in all the holy pride of Death-bed benevolence.

lence. It was valued, at the Dissolution, at the annual rent of two hundred and fifty-eight pounds: that property would now bring two thousand.

The dress of the Augustin order was a white surplice, girt round the waist, and extending to the knees, bordered with a broad lace. Over this, a black cloak tied under the chin, which hung loose to the feet; a cap of the same; their hair short. Henry the Eighth wisely thought, or rather Cromwell, that the most certain means of preventing the abbot from recovering his power, was to pull down his house.

The site of Derley, offspring of St. Helen's, was granted to Sir William West, who sold the tombs and the dust within them for twenty pounds; the cloister for ten; the chapter-house for one! noble pennyworths; which indicated the market was crowded with sellers, the purchasers few, and that holy relics were become a drug. Six bells in the steeple brought forty-five pounds one shilling and ten pence; the silver plate was 131 ounces. A small part of of this venerable building yet stands, in four divisions, but now recovered from ruins; one is part of a dwelling-house; two others are barns; and the fourth, part of a garden wall. I knew these ruins when they were much more considerable.

ST. MARY DE PRATIS,

A priory of Benedictine nuns. One of the rich abbots of St. Helen's founded this house in 1160, and endowed it. The Bishop of Coventry consecrated the young ladies who entered;—an act of greater beneficence, and more to their wish, had he procured them husbands. Many might be willing to enter upon a recluse life through novelty, but more to relinquish it when that novelty ceased. Man is made for society; not to hide himself from the world. This house stood one hundred yards Northwest of St. Mary's-mill (Nuns-mill), and twenty North of the bed of the old brook. The meadow bears the name of *Nuns Close,* is eight or nine acres, and is full of the vestiges of that religious foundation.

Henry the Third ordered the nuns to receive annually one hundred shillings from his fee-farm rent at Nottingham, to pray for the soul of his father King John.

Henry the Fourth, successor in honours to Ferrers Earl of Derby, in the first of his reign, granted to the nunnery of St. Mary de Pratis a charter, confirming all their emoluments.

In 1272, the nuns are said to have let three mills upon Hoddibrook (Markeatonbrook), at the annual rent of fourteen pounds and six marks; which I apprehend a mistake, no three in the kingdom could be worth that sum. They could not have been cheap at the odd six marks: these must have been Markeaton, St. Mary's, and Cuckstool mills. They possessed also the ground near the nunnery, valued at twenty shillings, perhaps 50 acres, and four carucates of land, 240 acres more. The whole, at the Dissolution, was valued at eighteen pounds, six shillings, and eight pence, *per annum.*

The

The dress of their order was a black gown which reached to the feet, with sleeves that would admit the body; a close cap covered the whole head, except the lower part of the face; it was bound under the chin, and descended upon the breast like a band. Over the head hung a black cloth, of the same materials as the gown, pending below the shoulders like the picture of Henry the Fourth. . Exclusive of this they wore a cowl.

DOMINICAN OR BLACK FRIARS.

Hence Friar-gate and Friar's-close. This was a priory dedicated to the Blessed Mary, whose name was stamped upon four or five places in Derby. The time of its foundation is uncertain, but must have been early. It is supposed to have stood about the middle of the close; and the chapel and cemetery upon the spot now Mr. Crompton's garden, because human bones were discovered; and the foundations of that gentleman's house were laid with stones from the priory.

The brotherhood multiplying, a patent was obtained in 1296 to enlarge its precincts, by the purchase of ten acres more.

At the Dissolution, the annual value was twenty-one pounds eighteen shillings and eight pence. The site was granted to John Hind. The destruction of religious houses, though founded in injustice, was the greatest benefit England ever experienced, as I have shewn in another work.

The habit of this order was a white robe, which hung to the feet; an apron of the same, a few inches shorter, girt round the waist; a black gown which descended to the bottom of the apron; a short black cloak with a hood; a fillet of hair surrounded the head, the crown being shaved, and always naked, except the monk chose to put up the hood.

ST. JAMES'S,

A priory on the North of St. James's-lane, adjoining the brook; an habitation of Cluniac Monks, which claims a Saxon origin.

origin. Walthof was an unfortunate nobleman, beheaded by William the Conqueror, in 1074, for supporting the rights of his country against tyranny, and was the first in England who fell by the axe. He gave this house to the abbey of Bermondsey in Southwark.

This priory, with the whole order, was subject to the abbey of Cluny in France. In the wars between Henry the Fifth and the French, they were all detached from the mother-abbey, our St. James's among the rest. This afterwards depended upon that of Lenton, near Nottingham, of the same order. It was protected by Henry the Third as a poor hospital; and at the Suppression was called the King's. Value ten pounds.

Coffins have been dug up, containing human bones, which, like the generality of old bones, were of an enormous size, as if, like a carrot, they grew in the earth.

This order of idle people appeared in a robe of black, much like that worn by a clergyman of the present day; to which

was

was added a hood of the same, with a cape covering the shoulders.

MAISON DE DIEU (HOUSE OF GOD) AND ST. LEONARD.

And now the Historian and the Reader will be lost together. We are entering a blind track, never trodden these 200 years; and Time has obliterated the guide-post.

The Authors who have written upon Religious Houses, tells us of two in Derby for Lepers; the Maison de Dieu, and St. Leonard's. If there were two, one must have been at the Newlands; the other at St. Mary's, Bridge-gate; because there are not the least traces of more. But I am inclined to think they are mistaken, and that these two are the same.

The place where this house stood is ascertained by an adjoining field, which bears the name of Abbey-barns. The house was in repute so early as Henry the Second's time.

ST. MARY'S.

There is no authority for supposing *this* a house for leprous persons; but, on the contrary, from the situation, the stile of the building, and the small light furnished by history, there is reason to conclude it never was appropriated to any religious use but that of a church. It is perfectly in the Saxon style, and was probably one of the six churches mentioned in Domesday. It stands upon the verge of the river, forms part of the bridge, with which it is interwoven, as if erected with it, and was in my time converted into little dwellings; these circumstances have, perhaps, prevented its total decay. It has not been used as a Church for ages, except during the small space mentioned above, in the reign of Charles the Second, by the Dissenters. In the days of its prosperity, Heanor was part of its appropriation.

Thus, my dear Reader, we have dived into the dark abodes of antiquity; if we have recovered as much hidden treasure as will pay you for reading, we shall both be satisfied; for I am amply paid in the pleasure derived from the research.

If we take a view of our progress, it will appear we have touched at six places, all sacred ground, set apart for holiness, famous for piety, expence, and miracle, and held in the highest veneration. But viewed in the present day, we may exclaim with Milton, " Alas, how changed!"—St. Helen's is an orchard: the fruit of the monastery is changed into that of the apple-tree; and however the ground, in two hundred years, may have lost its sacred influence, yet this fruit is as finely flavoured as if under the consecrating prayers of the monk.

That spot where the assemblage of the Fair composed a nunnery, where the practice of the life was not the wish of the heart; where the passions of the mind were suspended, and the designs of Nature inverted; is now laid in silence, except the noise of the winds blowing above, and the beast cropping the grass below. The place is is an open field, and Plenty smiles where Beauty wept.

Upon the resting-place of the Dominican Friar stands the noble mansion of a rich Banker; so that guineas rise where the monk was fed.

The spot over which the great St. James presided, was poor 600 years ago; it is poor still. *Under* the ground may be stone-coffins, and long bones; but above, are stables, poverty, and pig-sties.—The cloistered cypher of a man was less profitable than the brute.

The Abbey-barns, once the mournful scene of disease and complaint, was afterwards the joyful spot of my infant amusements.

Doubtful of another house of Lepers, I fly to St. Mary's, where munificence and devotion have given way to scolding and want; and the music of the vespers to the tumbling of the waters over the weirs.

TRADE.

TRADE.

The prosperity of a town depends upon its commerce; as that increases, knowledge, freedom, taste, luxury, power, and civilization, increase; perhaps we may also infuse into the composition a small degree of craft.

History is nearly silent on the trade of Derby; nor, till of late, had she much to record.

Perhaps the oldest occupation, whose produce exceeded the consumption of the place, was that of a *dyer*. This is corroborated by two evidences: an exclusive right, with Nottingham, derived from the old Lords of Derby, of *dying cloth;* and the name of *Full-street*, probably the residence of the professors of that art.

All the writers mention Derby as famous for *Ale;* consequently for drunkards; for the lower class ever want a little more than they can get.

Malt

Malt is another article for which she was famous. This was supplied from the barley-lands in the vicinity of Derby. The residue, after home consumption, was dispersed in small quantities in the Peak and Lancashire.

Wool also was among her articles of commerce. This was brought to market from the beautiful Sheep-walks of the Peak, and retailed in the neighbourhood; for though she bordered upon Yorkshire, she partook very little of the Northern manufactures; and I am inclined to think, the utmost success of these two trades barely enabled their professors to spread their tables with greater luxuries than two old-fashioned, but excellent dishes, pudding and beef.

Trade was in this confined situation during the lapse of many centuries, without much increase or diminution of the place; nor were the inhabitants poor during that long period; owing to a well-frequented market, which arose from the numerous villages in the vicinity. This brings us to the

the close of the seventeenth century.——
Those places where the manufactures flourish, draw, like a loadstone, the neighbouring inhabitants, and abound with males of the lower orders, so that we often behold a wife of sixteen; but Derby, having no internal commerce to retain her sons, they were diminished by emigration, or the military service; and the girls were left longing for husbands.

The next article of commerce which Derby experienced, was the productions of the *stocking-frame**.—We are told by tradition, that a Reverend Divine of Calverton, near Nottingham, about the reign

---

* "About 1756 Messrs. Jedediah Strutt and William Woollatt obtained a patent for making *ribbed* stockings. A common workman, named Roper, had furnished a rude idea of this useful machine; but it was left to the labour and ingenuity of the patentees, to bring it to perfection. The machinery is prefixed to the stocking-frame, and in connection with it produces ribbed stockings, similar to those knit with the knitting-needles. At present the manufacture of silk and cotton hose employs a great many hands in the town." DAVIES.

of James the First, paid his addresses to a Beauty, who kept a school to instruct young ladies in the art of knitting stockings. She disregarded his suit; which so provoked him, that he determined to put a period, not to *his* existence, like a desponding lover, but to her occupation; he therefore invented the stocking-frame, which enables the operator to perform the work of twenty knitters. Thus the art was founded in revenge, and revenge in love. In process of time the machine found its way into Derby, and promised to become a staple trade; but the silk-mill being introduced, and the wages tempting, it was foretold, " that the Hosiery would stagnate." The event verified the prediction; and *frames* are not more numerous than they were seventy years ago. There are about 150 in the place. Perhaps the loss was of no consequence to Derby, for the journeyman rather starves than lives: as if an employment founded in a diabolical passion entailed a curse upon the artist, by denying him bread.

There

There is also a decent, but unprofitable occupation, dependant upon the frame, in which near 300 of the fair sex are employed, *spinning jersey*. Here humble beauty is seen to toil for two and six-pence a week.

SILK MILL.

All the writers, who have travelled through Derby for half a century, from *Gregory* to *Gough*, give us a description of the *silk-mill*. But it is doubtful, whether an adequate idea can be formed of that wonderful machine, when described by an author who does not understand it himself. Some have earnestly wished to see this singular piece of mechanism; but I have sincerely wished I never had seen it. I have lamented, that while almost every man in the world was born *out* of Derby, it should be my unhappy lot to be born *in*. To this curious, but wretched place, I was bound apprentice for seven years, which I always considered

the

the most unhappy of my life; these I faithfully served; which was equalled by no other, in my time, except a worthy brother, then my companion in distress, and now my intelligent friend. It is therefore no wonder if I am perfectly acquainted with every movement in that superb work. My parents, through mere necessity, put me to labour before Nature had made me able. Low as the engines were, I was too short to reach them. To remedy this defect, a pair of high pattens were fabricated, and lashed to my feet, which I dragged after me till time lengthened my stature. The confinement and the labour were no burden; but the severity was intolerable, the marks of which I yet carry, and shall carry to the grave. The inadvertencies of an infant, committed without design, can never merit the extreme of harsh treatment. A love of power is predominant in every creature; a love to punish is often attendant upon that power. The man who delights in punishment is more likely to inflict it, than the offender to deserve it.

He

He who feels for another will not torture from choice. A merciful judge punishes with regret; a tyrant with pleasure. He who mourns over the chastisement he must inflict, will endeavour to reduce it; he who rejoices will augment it: one displays a great, the other a little mind. Hoisted upon the back of *Bryant Barker,* a giant approaching seven feet, was like being hoisted to the top of a precipice, when the wicked instrument of affliction was wielded with pleasure; but, alas, it was only a pleasure to one side. —It was again my unhappy lot, at the close of this servitude, to be bound apprentice to a stocking-maker, for a second seven years ; so that, like Jacob, I served two apprenticeships; but was not, like him, rewarded either with wealth or beauty. The time spent at the silk-mill is not included in the last fifty years. The erection of other mills has given a choice of place; and humanity has introduced a kinder treatment.

The Italians had the exclusive art of silk-throwing ; consequently an absolute command

command of that lucrative traffic. The wear of silks was the taste of the ladies; and the British merchant was obliged to apply to the Italian, with ready money, for the article, at an exorbitant price.

A gentleman of the name of Crotchet thought he saw a fine opening to raise a fortune; he therefore erected a small silk-mill in 1702, which joins the present work, and is called *The Old Shop*, now used for fabricating ornaments of the Derbyshire petrifactions. Every prospect of the future undertaking was favourable, till the scheme was put in practice, when the bright ideas died away. Three engines were found necessary for the whole process: he had but one. An untoward trade is a dreadful sink for money; and an imprudent tradesman is one more dreadful. We often see instances where a fortune would last a man much longer, if he lived upon his capital, than if he sent it into trade. Crotchet soon became insolvent.

John Lombe, a man of spirit, a good draughtsman, and an excellent mechanic,

M travelled

travelled into Italy, with a view of penetrating the secret. He staid some time; but as he knew admission was prohibited, he adopted the usual mode of accomplishing his end by corrupting the servants. This gained him frequent access in private. Whatever part he became master of, he committed to paper before he slept. By perseverance and bribery he acquired the whole, when the plot was discovered, and he fled, with the utmost precipitation, on board a ship, at the hazard of his life, taking with him two natives, who had favoured his interest and his life at the risk of their own. But though he judged the danger over, he was yet to become a sacrifice.

Arriving safe with his acquired knowledge, he fixed upon Derby as a proper place for his purpose, because the town was likely to supply him with a sufficient number of hands, and the able stream with a constant supply of water. This happened about the year 1717.

He

He agreed with the Corporation for an island or swamp in the river, five hundred feet long, and fifty-two wide, at eight pounds *per ann.* where he erected the present works, containing eight apartments, and 468 windows, at the expence of about £.30,000. This island, with another, called the Bye-flat, were part of the continent, but separated, ages past, by cutting two sluices to work four sets of mills. The ground continuing flat, farther West, would yet allow one or two sets more.

This ponderous building stands upon huge piles of oak, from sixteen to twenty feet long, driven close to each other with an engine made for that purpose. Over this solid mass of timber is laid a foundation of stone.

During three or four years, while this grand affair was constructing, he hired various rooms in Derby, and particularly the Town-hall, where he erected temporary engines, turned by hand. And although he reduced the prices so far below those of the Italians, as to monopolize the trade, yet the overflowings of profit were so very considerable, as to enable him to pay for the grand machine as the work went on.

It appears that the building was compleated, and in full employ, several years before the leases were executed, which was not done till 1724, and extended to seventy-nine years.

Being established to his wish, he procured in 1718 a patent from the crown, to secure the profits during fourteen years. But, alas! he had not pursued this lucrative commerce more than three or four years, when the Italians, who felt the effects of the theft from their want of trade, determined *his* destruction, and hoped that of his works would follow.

An artful woman came over in the character of a friend, associated with the parties, and assisted in the business. She attempted to gain both the Italians, and succeeded with one. By these two, slow poison was supposed, and perhaps justly,

to

to have been administered to John Lombe, who lingered two or three years in agonies, and departed. The Italian ran away to his own country; and Madam was interrogated, but nothing transpired except what strengthened suspicion.

Grand funerals were the fashion; and John Lombe's was, perhaps, the most superb ever known in Derby. A man of a peaceable deportment, who had brought a beneficial manufactory into the place, employed the poor, and at advanced wages, could not fail to meet with respect, and his melancholy end with pity. Exclusive of the gentlemen who attended, all the people concerned in the works were invited. The procession marched in pairs, and extended the length of Full-street, the Market-place, and Iron-gate; so that when the corpse entered All Saints, at St. Mary-gate, the last couple left the house of the deceased, at the corner of Silk-mill-lane. Besides a row of flambeaux on each side of the procession, one person in every fourth couple carried a branch, with four candles, weighing a pound.

Though

Though the unhappy victim died at the early age of twenty-nine, and by a cruel death, yet the priest who preached his funeral-sermon took for his text, " He is brought to his grave as a shock of corn in its season."—There is, however, a remark in favour of this ill-chosen text: the good never quit the world *out* of season.

John dying a bachelor, his property fell into the hands of his brother William, who enjoyed, or rather possessed the works but a short time; for, being of a melancholy turn, he shot himself. This superb erection, therefore, became the property of his cousin, Sir Thomas Lombe. I believe this happened about the year 1726.

If the Italians destroyed the man, they miscarried in their design upon the works; for they became more successful, and continued to employ about 300 people.

In 1732 the patent expired; when Sir Thomas, a true picture of human nature, petitioned Parliament for a renewal, and pleaded, " That the works had taken so long a time in perfecting, and the people

in

in teaching, that there had been none to acquire emolument from the patent." But he forgot to inform them that he had already accumulated more than £.120,000. thus veracity flies before profit. It is, however, no wonder disguise should appear at St. Stephen's, where the heart and the tongue so often disagree.

Government, willing to spread so useful an invention, gave Sir Thomas £.14,000 to suffer the trade to be open, and a model of the works taken. This is deposited in the Tower, and considered as one of the greatest curiosities there.

A mill was immediately erected at Stockport, in Cheshire, which drew many of the workmen from that of Derby, and, among others, Nathaniel Gartrevalli, the remaining Italian, who, sixteen years before, had come over with John Lombe : him I personally knew; he ended his days in poverty; the frequent reward of the man who ventures his life in a base cause, or betrays his country.

Since then eleven mills have been erected

in

in Derby*, and silk is now the staple trade of the place: more than a thousand hands are said to be employed in the various works, but they are all upon a diminutive scale compared to this.

The describers of this elaborate work tell us mechanically, as followers of the first author, that " it contains 26,000 wheels, 97,000 movements, which work 71,000 yards of silk-thread, while the water-wheel, which is eighteen feet high, makes one revolution, and that three are performed in a minute. That one fire-engine conveys warmth to every individual part of the machine; and that one regulator governs the whole."—By these wholesale numbers, the Reader is left about as wise as before. The design of writing is to communicate the

* " The mills established by Messrs. Strutts, for the manufacture of silk and cotton, are particularly ingenious; and the facility attained by them in working the several articles of manufacture, has contributed to the extension of these branches of business in a very eminent degree." DAVIES.

same

same intelligence to the understanding, as might be conveyed through the eye or the ear, upon the spot.—Had the Author made the number of his *wheels* 10,000 less, he would have been nearer the mark; or if he had paid an unremitting attendance for seven years, he might have found their number 13,384. Perhaps his *movements*, an indeterminate word, will also bear a large discount; but as I am neither in the humour to calculate nor contradict, I shall leave him in possession of his own authority. What number of *yards* are wound, every circuit of the wheel, no man can tell; nor is the number open to calculation. The wheel revolves about *twice* in a minute. Nor is the superb *fire-engine*, which blazes in description, any more than a common stove, which warmed *one corner* of that large building, and left the others to starve: but the defect is now supplied by fire-places. The *regulator* is a peg in the master-wheel, which strikes a small bell every revolution: near it is a pendulum, which vibrates about fifty times in a minute.

Twenty-

Twenty-four returns of the pendulum is the medium velocity of the wheel.—Although there are a vast number of parts, any one of which may be stopped, and separated at pleasure; yet the whole, extending through five large rooms, is *one* regular machine, which moves and stops together. Every minute part is attended with two wheels, one of which turns the other. If you separate the two, the last stops of course, while the former moves gently on.

The raw silk is brought in hanks, or skaines, called slips, which would take five or six days in winding off, though kept moving ten hours a day. Some are the produce of Persia; others of Canton, coarse, and in small slips; some are from Piedmont, these are all of a yellowish colour; and some are from China, perfectly white. The work passes through three different engines; one to wind; the second to twist; and the third to double. Though the thread is fine, it is an accumulation of many. The workman's care is chiefly to unite, by a knot, a thread that breaks; to
take

take out the burs and uneven parts, some of which are little bags, fabricated by the silk-worm, as a grave for itself, when Nature inspires the idea of leaving the world: the bags are neatly closed up, and hung to a thread, as the last efforts towards its own funeral. They generally moulder to a darkish dust; sometimes the worms are totally gone: but I have frequently taken them out alive. The threads are continually breaking; and to tye them is principally the business of children whose fingers are nimble. The machine continually turns a round bobbin, or small block of wood, which draws the thread from the slip, while expanded upon a swift, suspended on a centre. The moment the thread breaks, the swift stops. One person commands from twenty to sixty threads. If many cease, at the same time, to turn, it amounts to a fault, and is succeeded by punishment. From the fineness of the materials, the ravelled state of the slips and bobbins, and the imprudence of children, much waste is made, which is another motive of correction;

tion; and when correction is often inflicted, it steels the breast of the inflictor.

NAVIGATION.

Although few places are more subject to floods, yet there are few that can enjoy equal benefit from a watery situation. This verifies the old adage, " There is no evil without its good." While the two rivers run smiling on, they seem to say to the inhabitants of Derby, " We are well adapted for the manufactures; use us with caution, and we will serve you. Riches for the master, and employment for the servant, may be drawn from our sources."

The noble river of Derwent ran useless for ages. No wheel was turned by its powers; no barge floated upon its surface. But in later ages it has, in some degree, been applied to the use of man.——An act was obtained in 1719 to make it navigable to the town; which opened the markets for heavy goods, such as were before excluded through bad roads and expensive

pensive conveyance. This produced a singular benefit, by taking off a redundancy, procuring the articles wanted at an easy price, and finding employment for the workman.

SLITTING, ROLLING, AND BATTERING MILLS.

In 1734 an additional advantage was derived from the Derwent, by erecting the slitting-mills at the Holmes, which prepare iron for various uses. And about three years after, another near them for smelting, rolling, and preparing copper for sheathing the Navy. These perhaps are not the last the river will work.

PORCELAIN

Began about the year 1750 *. There is only one manufactory, which employs

---

* " By a gentleman of the name of Duesbury. Since the decease of the original institutor, very great improvements have been made, in the preparation

about seventy* people. The clay is not
of equal fineness with the foreign, but the

ration of the materials, and in the appearance of
the ware. It is thought to be equal in fineness of
texture with the French and Saxon, while it far
surpasses them in workmanship, and elegance.—
The paintings are in general rich and well executed; and the gilding and burnishing very beautiful.

"The materials from which the ware, called porcelain, is manufactured, is procured from Cornwall; and is a fine grey clay, mixed with fluxing
matter. These materials first undergo the operation of grinding, and then are made into a paste;
which, when it is perfected, is taken to the workmen, who form it into a variety of useful and ornamental articles. Vessels of a round shape, are
formed by a person called a *thrower;* who shapes
them on a circular block, moving horizontally on a
vertical spindle. They are then taken to a lathe,
where they are reduced to their proper thickness,
and afterwards finished and handled. When this
process is gone through, they are conveyed to a
stove to dry, and when all the moisture is evaporated, they become fit for baking. The ware is
placed in earthen vessels, of different shapes and

* It now employs about 200 persons. EDIT.

dimensions,

workmanship exceeds it. The arts of
drawing and engraving have much im-

dimensions, among a white sand, to prevent their adhering to one another; and set in a kiln or oven, piled one on another to the top. When the kiln is full, the apertures are carefully closed, and the ware baked by the heat proceeding from the flues. After the ware has undergone this first baking, it is taken to another apartment, where it is dipped in a glaze of the colour and consistence of cream: it is then taken to the *glaze-kiln*, where it is baked in a less intense heat than the former, and receives its glossy appearance.

After the ware has been glazed, it is taken to the painters, who ornament it with landscapes, figures, &c. The colours used are prepared from mineral bodies; and in order to fix, and give them a proper degree of lustre, they are conveyed to a kiln, where every coat of colour receives a fresh burning. Two burnings are generally sufficient for the ornaments of common porcelain; but the most elegant ware, has the colours laid on at different periods, and therefore require the action of fire several times, before they attain their full effect and beauty. When the ware is ornamented with gold, that metal is used in an amalgamated state, and laid on by a brush: in this case, it is necessary to commit the vessel once more to the kiln, where the gold re-assumes its solidity, and being rubbed

after

proved within these last thirty years. The improvements of the porcelain have kept pace with these. They adhere to Nature in their designs; to which the Chinese have not attained. A desert service of 120 after it comes out, with some polishing substance, acquires a brilliant appearance.

At this manufactory, many very elegant *biscuit figures*, or white ware, are constructed.—The materials for the construction of these figures, are reduced to a liquid of the consistence and appearance of thick cream, and then poured into moulds of plaster or gypsum.—The moisture contained in the mixture, being very soon absorbed by the mould, the paste which composes the figure, becomes hard and tenacious, and easily separates. The different parts of the figure; the head, the arms, the legs, and numerous other appendages, which belong to many of them, are cast in separate moulds, and when dried, and prepared, are joined to the principal figure, by a paste of the same kind as the figure itself. When the figures have their limbs, &c. complete, they are conveyed to the kiln, and by the operation of a regulated and continued heat, are rendered beautifully white and delicate. They then undergo the same process as the other ware in laying on the different colours. The manufactory belongs at present to Messrs. Duesbury and Key." DAVIES.

pieces was recently fabricated here for the Prince of Wales.

The spot upon which this elegant building stands, which is internally replete with taste and utility, was once the freehold of my family. It cost thirty-five pounds: but the purchaser, my grandfather's brother, being unable to raise more than twenty-eight, mortgaged it for seven. Infirmity, age, and poverty, obliged him to neglect the interest; when, in 1743, it fell into the hands of my father, as heir at law, who, being neither able nor anxious to redeem it, conveyed away his right to the mortgagee for a guinea.

JEWELLERY.

This trade began to take root about the same time as the porcelain, and grew to some magnitude; but the change of fashions caused its lustre to fade. Diamonds may never be out of use, but their imitations may; these being little worn, the trade decays.

SPAR.

This is another recent manufactory* in Derby arising from the internal riches of

* Carried on by Messrs. Brown and Son. "The machinery employed here, which is novel and simple, but very ingenious, is set in motion by a large steam-engine. The machinery for sawing and polishing the marble, consists of a set of saws, made of thin plates of iron, inclosed in a sliding frame, attached to the vibrating poles to which the cranks are fixed. These saws, by the assistance of sand and water, cut the marble in a perpendicular direction. A set of saws consists of many plates, so that the block to which they are applied, may be separated by one process into as many slabs as may be thought necessary. When the slabs are sawn, they are taken to be polished by an equally ingenious method.

" When the *Blue John* is to be made into a vase, or any other ornamental form, that renders the use of the lathe necessary, it is carved with a mallet and chissel, into a rude resemblance of the object intended to be produced, and being afterwards strongly cemented to a plug or *chock*, is screwed upon the lathe. A slow motion is then given to the work; and a bar of steel, about two feet long, and

half

the Peak. The substances are of the most exquisite beauty, and curiously modelled into a variety of ornamental forms for halls, windows, chimney-pieces, &c.; also for candlesticks, snuff-boxes, and daily new inventions. The stranger cannot pass a shop, where these elegant ornaments are displayed, without having his eye arrested, and his mind delighted. Here he sees captivating Nature improved by Art.

half an inch square, properly tempered, and pointed at each end, is applied to the fluor, on which water is continually dropping, to keep the tool cold, preserve it from friction, and enable it the more readily to reduce the substance upon which it acts. As the surface becomes smoother, the tool is applied with more freedom, and the motion of the lathe accelerated, till the fluor has assumed its destined elegance of form. When the turning is completed, pieces of grit-stone, of different degrees of fineness, are applied with water to bring the article to a proper ground for polishing with fine emery, tripoli, and putty, or calx of tin. These means are continued till the fluor is incapable of receiving a higher degree of polish; which is known, when water thrown on it will no longer increase its lustre." DAVIES.

COTTON.

The introduction of this manufactory is of much later date. Two machines upon the Arkwright plan add to the modern commerce; and several looms have lately been constructed for the fabrication of calicoes.—Another machine, still later, appeared, to convert wool into a thread for weaving carpets.

From the above state of trade in Derby, it appears that she crept silently through ages without much connexion with Commerce, except what arose from her own taylors, hatters, weavers, and shoe-makers, till the beginning of the present century, when the frame, the river, the silk-mill, the porcelain, &c. awakened her drowsy talents to riches, increase, and notice. The man who has known her threescore years can easily discover an improvement in her external buildings, and the extension of her borders. He may as easily prophecy, that, like an infant, whose

whose powers are equal to its magnitude, it can stand upon its own basis, and will rise more rapidly towards maturity.

" Besides the above-mentioned manufactures, several others are carried on to a considerable extent· There is a small bleaching-mill situated on Nun's-green, where the processes are performed, according to the improved chemical methods: and to aid its operations, a small steam-engine has been erected. A mill for slitting and rolling iron, for various purposes; a large furnace for smelting copper ore, with a machine for battering and rolling the copper into sheets; a red-lead mill; a mill for making tinned plates; and an extensive shot-mill; are to be found in the town, or in its immediate vicinity*."

AMUSEMENTS.

Man, as a changeable animal, requires as much variety of action as of food. Even

* Davies's History of Derbyshire, p. 174.

the most desirable weather, pursuits, diet, or pleasure, tires.

Some of the amusements of Derby are common with those of other places. Some are local. Recreations should always be inoffensive : they may be divided into two classes, the *mental* and corporeal. The first is chiefly adopted by the more refined ranks of men, and consists in *conversation*, which is much cultivated here, by small clubs or societies, in nocturnal meetings. In these well-regulated associations are united entertainment and improvement.— *In reading:* the man who has no relish for letters, must, in some idle moments, be a burden to himself. To converse with the dead is the next pleasure to that of conversing with the living: both form the man. This pleasure is well known in Derby. Men of reading not only abound, but there are many book-societies who keep pace with the press.— A third mental amusement is that of the *stage*. This is a garden of weeds and flowers; the man of sense well knows which to chuse : he can distin-

guish

guish the sentiment from the sound. He will sometimes reverse the intention of the Poet and the Player; for the Comedy, with a tender thought, may excite a tear, and the unnatural Tragedy, disgust. This is an amusement cultivated in Derby; and a spacious theatre, recently erected, is a proof of the taste of the inhabitants.

One of the corporeal entertainments is found in an elegant *assembly-room*, chiefly confined to the younger and more elevated class. To lead the *hand* of the Fair is an introduction towards leading the heart; for the hand is not the only part affected by pressure. This kind of assemblage tends to soften the temper and refine the manners.

All the above amusements are found upon *land;* but there are two which are local, and arise from the water, *fishing* and *swimming*. The inhabitants are adepts in both.

There is also one amusement of the amphibious kind, which, if not peculiar to Derby, is pursued with an avidity I have not observed elsewhere, *foot-ball*. I have

seen

seen this coarse sport carried to the barbarous height of an election-contest; nay, I have known a foot-ball hero chaired through the streets like a successful member, although his utmost elevation of character was no more than that of a butcher's apprentice. Black eyes, bruised arms, and broken shins, are equally the marks of victory and defeat. I need not say this is the delight of the lower ranks, and is attained at an early period; the very infant learns to *kick*, and then to walk. The professors of this athletic art think themselves bound to follow the ball wherever it flies; and, as Derby is fenced in with rivers, it seldom flies far without flying into the water; and I have seen these amphibious practitioners of foot-ball-kicking jump into the river upon a Shrove-Tuesday when the ground was covered with snow. Whether the benefits arising from exercise pay for the bloody nose is doubtful; whether this rough pastime improves the mind, I leave to the decision of its votaries; and whether the wounds in youth produce the pains in age, I leave to threescore.

OCCURRENCES.

As Derby never figured in history, remarkable events cannot abound; they have slept with Time. When they happened, like value in possession, they were disregarded: but a value arises and increases with years. There may also have been no hand to record them. One of the uses of History is faithfully to bring the *past* to the present.

874. The first memorable event mentioned in history, is our fore-fathers, those dreadful plunderers, the Danes, whom no distress could move, no treaties bind, approaching Mercia, under Halfden, their prince. Their head-quarters for the winter were at Reppendune (Repton), eight miles from Derby, then much larger than at present. They occupied all the neighbouring places; the whole country was kept in subjection; and Derby, though never a fortified place, was the residence of a considerable part of that army of freebooters.
The

The castle was its only place of strength, which was garrisoned by Halfden's forces.

918. During the long and bloody contest between the Danes and the Saxons, Derby frequently changed its master. The Danes chiefly inhabited the North of England; and the Saxons the South. They approached each other through Derby, as the medium, which often felt the horrors of robbery and butchery. The dread of their cruelties continued upon the mind for ages; nay, it was not totally worn off even so late as my infancy; the elder child, already frightened, informed the younger, " that the Danes would arrive, enter every house, and murder all the people."

Alfred the Great left several children. His son, called Edward the Elder, mounted the throne in 900. A daughter, named Ethelfleda, married Ethelred Earl of Mercia. Their residence was Tamworth-castle. She was said to have undergone so much danger and pain in child-birth, that she made a vow to renounce the embraces of her husband, and devote herself to arms; which

which perhaps was true; for she was a masculine character, better adapted to *reduce* than *augment* the race. This is certain: she never contradicted herself by bringing a second child; and though her husband died about the year 908, she never took another to publish a broken vow. She was firmly attached to her brother Edward, who was at war with the Danes from 910 to 922. While they were in possession of Derby in 918, she saw an opening to revenge her brother's wrongs and her own. Having mustered a body of English forces, she privately marched into Derby, at the passage now St. Mary's-bridge, attacked the enemy by surprize, and totally routed them. This battle, no doubt, was fought in the streets; and the retiring army was driven to the castle, which was quickly taken, and most of the enemy put to the sword. The Danes, though in confusion, must have fought bravely, as Ethelfleda lost many of her people, and four of her principal officers, whom she much regarded, not as men, but as heroes.—This unhappy

unhappy place was soon recovered by its former masters.

944. King Edmund the First took from Anlaff, a Danish prince, Derby, Nottingham, Leicester, Lincoln, and Stafford, with the small intermediate places.

1514. Sir William Milnes, the judge, was obliged to hold the assizes at the market-cross, which proves there was one. Perhaps there was no hall.

1554. Sir John Marriott, vicar of St. Alkmund's, hanged himself in one of the bell-ropes. We are not told from what cause; but if *Sir John* was condemned to starve upon a benefice of eight pounds a year, no wonder he sought a reprieve in the belfry.

1572. The townsmen played Holofernes—the stage then exhibited none but religious subjects.

1586. The plague visited St. Peter's parish.

1587. A remarkable flood broke down St. Mary's-bridge, and carried away the mills at the bottom of St. Michael's-lane.

1590. Edward Smith's corn was destroyed

in

in the Siddals. Edward Smith was one of the Corporation; the Siddals was burgesses land; and he perhaps had bargained with his brethren for the place, which the freemen would not suffer him to possess.

1595. Sir Thomas White gave four hundred pounds to the town.

1601. Two hundred soldiers, marching through Derby from Lincolnshire to Ireland, quarrelled with the towns-people while going to prayers.—A woman burnt in Windmill-pit, for poisoning her husband.

1603. Some of the common grounds being inclosed, the fences were broken down by the burgesses; several persons were indicted, and suffered imprisonment. These common grounds, I apprehend, lie between St. Alkmund's and Derley, upon the banks of the Derwent.

1608. The witches of Bakewell were executed. Nor is it a wonder that innocence should suffer, under that weak and witch-ridden monarch, James the First.

1610. So violent a quarrel took place between the electioneering parties of Sir Philip

Philip Stanhope and Sir George Gresley, of two ancient families in the neighbourhood, that the Assizes were held at Ashborn.—By a sudden rise of the brook, three prisoners in the jail were drowned.

1615. Mrs. Walker died, and was carried to the grave by her four sons, all brethren in the Corporation.

1634. A great snow, wherein four persons perished between Chaddesdon and Derby.

1635. Charles the First was at Derby, and slept at the great house in the Market-place. The Corporation gave the Duke of Newcastle, for the King, a fat ox, a calf, six fat sheep, and a purse of gold, to enable him to keep hospitality; that is, invite them to dinner; and to the Elector Palatine, his brother, twenty broad pieces.

1636. The plague appeared in Bag-lane.

1642. When Charles the First set up his standard at Nottingham, about twenty Derby men marched there, and entered his service.

1643.

1643. The King marched through Derby, and borrowed three hundred pounds of the Corporation, with all the arms they could procure, and promised to return both; but never had the power to do either. In November Sir John Gell garrisoned the town for the Parliament, and kept the main guard at the town-hall.

1645. The town was dis-garrisoned. The Assizes were held in Friar's Close, owing to the plague being in Derby.—Richard Cockrum was executed at the gallows on Nuns-green, for killing ------- Mills, a servant at the Angel.

1650. Caddows houses burnt at the top of Bridge-gate.

1659. An insurrection was raised against the government of one of the best of men, Richard Cromwell, who cheerfully gave up, without blood, what he had no right to keep.

Assiduity merits a relaxation; even the Divine who harangues the world for an hour, may fairly be allowed a small interval to step into his own house, and arrange the

trifles

trifles of his family.—A regiment of troopers in 1647, in the Parliament's service, marching over St. Mary's-bridge, in their way to Nottingham, observed a girl of fifteen, a few yards below the bridge, lading water into her pail while standing upon a *Bating-lag* (beating-log, upon which the dyer stands to beat his cloth); some soldierly jokes ensued, when one of them dismounted, and cast a large stone, with a design to splash her; but not being versed in directing a stone so well as a bullet, he missed the water, and broke her head. Alarmed at this unexpected result of his rude attack, he hastened to the front of the regiment to avoid the consequence: thus the man, who had boldly faced an enemy in the field, fled with fear from a helpless female. Nothing disarms like offered injuries. She instantly, with cries and tears, left her pail, and went home, where her mother was frightened to behold her covered with a stream of blood. The unknown consequences of this adventure hung upon the trooper's mind: he rode in the regiment

ment eleven years after. When discharged, the world being all before him where to chuse, he fixed at Derby, followed his occupation, courted and married a young woman. In the course of their conversations, he proved to be the very man who cast the stone, and she the woman with the broken head. They lived in Bridge-gate, and in harmony, about 30 years: during that period they produced ten children, the eldest of whom was my grandfather.—His sword, in my possession, was drawn for liberty at Marston-moor, under the Earl of *Manchester;* at Naseby, under *Fairfax;* and at Worcester under *Cromwell;* and was carried in pursuit of the unfortunate Charles to Boscobel.

1660. The present mace was made, which is elegant: till now the Mayor had two old ones, formerly used by the bailiffs.

1661. The Derwent was dried up. People walked over the bed of the river dryshod.—The hall was regulated; and Mr. Degge (Sir Simon), chosen recorder.

1662.

1662. A terrible hurricane blew up trees, broke down the pinnacle of St. Warburgh's steeple, untiled the town-hall, and many houses in the Market-place, Full-street, and other places on the South of All Saints; but on the North, not a tile, or scarcely a straw was moved.—Edward Smith's wife drowned herself at St. James's-bridge: a young child in her arms was carried down the stream to a sand-bed, against Alderman Spateman's door; where, recovering breath, it cried, was taken up, and saved.

1665. Derby was again visited by the plague at the same time in which London fell under that severe calamity. The town was forsaken; the farmers declined the Market-place; and grass grew upon that spot which had furnished the supports of life. To prevent a famine, the inhabitants erected at the top of Nuns-green, one or two hundred yards from the buildings, now Friar-gate, what bore the name of *Head-less-cross*, consisting of about four quadrangular steps, covered in the centre with one large

large stone; the whole near five feet high;
I knew it in perfection. Hither the market-
people, having their mouths primed with
tobacco as a preservative, brought their
provisions, stood at a distance from their
property, and at a greater from the towns-
people, with whom they were to traffic.
The buyer was not suffered to touch any of
the articles before purchase; but when the
agreement was finished, he took the goods,
and deposited the money in a vessel filled
with vinegar, set for that purpose. A con-
fidence, raised by necessity, took place between buyer and seller, which never existed
before or since; the first could not examine
the value of his purchase, nor the second
that of his money. Such were the pre-
cautions taken by our forefathers against
one of the most dreadful enemies of man
A small part of this cross is yet visible,
joining the prison. It was observed, that
this cruel affliction never attempted the
premises of a tobacconist, a tanner, or a
shoe-maker.—A woman was pressed to
death in the county-hall as a mute.

1673.

1673. A great flood upon Markeaton-brook, carried away the hay, filled the cellars as high as the Angel (Rotten-row), and broke down three of the ten bridges. St. James's bridge was landed at the Sun in St. Peter's parish.

1674. The apprentices and others assembled, pulled down, and burnt the fences of Henry Mellor's intakes, in Little-field and Castle-field. Some of the rioters were imprisoned, tried, and fined six-and-eight-pence each.

1675. A quarrel between Henry Mellor and the Corporation caused about forty law-suits relative to the above inclosure.—A fire at Northampton destroyed most of the town. The inhabitants of Derby, out of compassion, sent them one hundred and fifty pounds; and Mr. Grey, their town-clerk, twenty.

1676. We sometimes behold that singularity of character which joyfully steps out of the beaten track for the sake of being ridiculous; thus the Barber, to excite attention, exhibited in his window green, blue, and

and yellow wigs; and thus *Noah Bullock*, enraptured with his name, that of the first navigator, and the founder of the largest family upon record, having three sons, named them after those of his predecessor, Shem, Ham, and Japhet: and to complete the farce, being a man of property, he built an ark, and launched it upon the Derwent, above St. Mary's-bridge; whether a *Bullock* graced the stern, history is silent. Here Noah and his sons enjoyed their abode, and the world their laugh. But nothing is more common than for people to deceive each other. The world acts under a mask. If *they* publicly ridiculed him, he privately laughed at them: for it afterwards appeared, he had more sense than honesty; and more craft than either; for this disguise and retreat were to be a security to coin money. He knew Justice could not easily overtake him; and if it should, the *deep* was ready to hide his crimes and utensils. Sir Simon Degge, an active magistrate, who resided at Babington-hall, was informed of *Noah's* proceedings, whom he personally knew:
the

the Knight sent for him, and told him, "he had taken up a new occupation, and desired to see a specimen of his work." Noah hesitated. The magistrate promised that no evil should ensue, provided he relinquished the trade. He then pulled out a sixpence, and told Sir Simon, "He could make as good work as that." The Knight smiled; Noah withdrew, broke up his ark, and escaped the halter.

1680. The association of the inhabitants to preserve their rights against the incroachments of the Crown was burnt. Charles the Second rode triumphant upon the liberties of the people; the old charter was surrendered; and the present procured at the expence of four hundred pounds.

1688. The Earl of Devonshire arrived with 500 men, invited the gentlemen of the town to dinner, declared for the Prince of Orange, and read the Prince's declaration; but, however well they might wish the interest, they refused to join. — A detachment of the Prince's troops afterwards entering, the Mayor, John Cheshire, durst not

not billet them, perhaps through sentiment more than fear: however, a spirited constable of the name of Cook sent them into quarters.

1705. *John Crosland.*

There is not a more pleasing feature in the human mind, than that of *love to man.* There is not one more beneficial. He who has this amiable quality, never gives a just cause of offence. His maxim is, to do good to all he can, but injury to none. Nor is this a rare character, notwithstanding the depravity of the age proclaimed from the pulpit. I know numbers of this description; and some of them I have every day the pleasure of conversing with. Such a temper carries its own reward, by bringing happy returns to its possessor. It is also delightful to an historian when he can work with such valuable materials. But he has no choice of subject; faithfulness binds him to accept indiscriminately whatever offers; if he cast the hook, he must take the bite, however disgusting. I have caught one of the most despicable of animals in the human form, and must give him to the Reader.

About

About the reign of Oliver Cromwell, or the beginning of Charles the Second, a whole family, consisting of a father and two sons, of the name of *Crosland,* were tried at Derby Assizes, and condemned, I think, for horse-stealing. As the offence was not capital, the Bench, after sentence, entertained the cruel whim of extending mercy to one of the criminals, but upon this barbarous condition, that the pardoned man should hang the other two. When Power wantons in cruelty, it becomes detestable, and gives greater offence than even the culprits. The offer was made to the father, being the senior. As distress is the season for reflection, he replied with meekness, " Was it ever known that a father hanged his children? How can I take away those lives which I have given, have cherished, and which, of all things, are the most dear?"—He bowed, declined the offer, and gave up his life. Barbarous Judges! I am sorry I cannot transmit their names to posterity. This noble reply ought to have pleaded his pardon. It

was

was then made to the eldest son, who trembling answered, " Though life is the most valuable of all possessions, yet even *that* may be purchased too dear. I cannot consent to preserve my existence by taking away him who gave it; nor could I face the world, or even myself, should I be left the only branch of that family which I had destroyed." Love, tenderness, compassion, and all the appendages of honour, must have associated in returning this answer. The proposition was then of course made to the younger, John, who accepted it with an avidity that seemed to tell the Court, he would hang half the creation, and even his judges, rather than be a sufferer himself.— He performed the fatal work, without remorse, upon his father and brother, in which he acquitted himself with such dexterity, that he was appointed to the office of hangman in Derby, and two or three neighbouring counties, and continued it to extreme age. So void of feeling for distress, he rejoiced at a murder, because it brought the prospect

of

of a guinea. Perhaps he was the only man in court who could hear with pleasure a sentence of death. The bodies of the executed were his perquisite: signs of life have been known to return after execution; in which case, he prevented the growing existence by violence. Loving none, and beloved by none, he spent a life of enmity with man. The very children pelted him in the streets. The mothers endeavoured to stop the infant cry with the name of *John Crosland;* and I have the irksome task of recording him.—He died without regret about the year 1705.

1715 produced frequent riots in favour of the abdicated House of Stuart. Personal insults and broken windows were the result. This wild-fire was fed with combustibles from the pulpit: that spot, which ought to have corrected the errors of man, brought them into action. Sturges, of All Saints, prayed publicly for *King James;* but after a moment's reflection, "*I mean King George.*" The congregation became tumultuous; the military gentlemen

gentlemen drew their swords, and ordered him out of the pulpit, into which he never returned. He pleaded *a slip of the tongue;* but if he had dipped into the New Testament, he might have sheltered himself under a better excuse, for we are there commanded *to pray for our enemies.* Harris, of St. Peter's, was repeatedly called to order by the powerful voice of the Magistrates. Cantril, of St. Alkmund's, drank the Pretender's health upon his knees; and the thirtieth of January became the most holy day in the year. But the wiser Lockett, of St. Michael's, rather chose to amuse himself with mowing his grass-plat, than meddling with politics.

1732. There are characters who had rather amuse the world, at the hazard of their lives, for a slender and precarious pittance, than follow an honest calling for an easy subsistence. A small figure of a man, of the name of Cadman, seemingly composed of spirit and gristle, appeared in October, to entertain the town by sliding down a rope. One end of this was to be

fixed

fixed at the top of All Saints steeple; and the other at the bottom of St. Michael's; an horizontal distance of eighty yards, which formed an inclined plain extremely steep. A breast-plate of wood, with a groove to fit the rope, and his own equilibrium, were to be his security, while sliding down upon his belly, with his arms and legs extended. He could not be more than six or seven seconds in this airy journey, in which he fired a pistol and blew a trumpet. The velocity with which he flew, raised a fire by friction, and a bold stream of smoke followed him. He performed this wonderful exploit three successive days, in each of which he descended twice, and marched up once; the latter took him more than an hour, in which he exhibited many surprizing achievements, as sitting unconcerned with his arms folded, lying across the rope upon his back, then his belly, his hams, blowing the trumpet, swinging round, hanging by the chin, the hand, the heels, the toe, &c. The rope being too long for art to tighten, he might be be said to have danced upon the slack. Though he succeeded at Derby, yet, in exhibiting soon after at Shrewsbury, he fell, and lost his life.

Feats of activity are sure to catch the younger part of the world. No amusement was seen but the rope; walls, posts, trees, and houses, were mounted for the pleasure of flying down: if a straggling scaffold pole could be found, it was reared for the convenience of flying; nay, even cats, dogs, and things inanimate, were applied, in a double sense, to the rope.

This flying rage was not cured till August, 1734, when another diminutive figure appeared, much older than the first: with a coat in dishabille; no waistcoat; shirt and shoes the worse for wear; a hat worth three-pence, exclusive of the band, which was packthread bleached by the weather; and a black string supplying the place of buttons to his waistband. He wisely considered, that if his performances did not exceed the other's, he might as well stay at home, if he had one. His rope,

rope, therefore, from the same steeple extended to the bottom of St. Mary-gate, more than twice the former length. He was to draw a wheel-barrow after him, in which was a boy of thirteen. After this surprizing performance, an ass was to fly down, armed as before, with a breast-plate, and at each foot a lump of lead about half a hundred weight. The man, the barrow, and its contents, arrived safe at the end of their journey; when the vast multitude turned their eyes towards the ass, which had been braying several days at the top of the steeple for food; but, like many a lofty courtier for a place, brayed in vain. The slackness of the rope, and the great weight of the animal and his apparatus, made it seem, at setting off, as if he was falling perpendicular. The appearance was tremendous! About twenty yards before he reached the gates of the countyhall, the rope broke: from the velocity acquired by the descent he bore down all before him. A whole multitude was overwhelmed; nothing was heard but dreadful

dreadful cries; nor seen, but confusion. Legs and arms went to destruction. In this dire calamity, the ass, which maimed others, was unhurt himself, having a pavement of soft bodies to roll over. No lives were lost. As the rope broke near the top, it brought down both chimnies and people at the other end of the street.——This dreadful catastrophe put a period to the art of flying. It prevented the operator from making the intended collection; and he sneaked *out* of Derby as poor as he sneaked in.

1732. John Hewit was a butcher, about thirty, of a moderately fair character, had been married about seven years, was blessed with one daughter, and resided in Stepping-lane; but *he* wanting that regard for his wife which is requisite for happiness, and *she* that prudence necessary to secure his affection, they lived upon ill terms. The same conduct which at first diminishes love, will in time annihilate it. This was the case with our unhappy couple. He treated her with neglect, with violence, and a diminution

nution of sustenance; and she sought relief in intoxication.

Eleanor Beare was a handsome woman, about the same age, with an education superior to her rank, and was mistress of that persuasive eloquence which insensibly wins over the hearer to her own side. She kept a paltry public-house, the White-Horse, nearly opposite the present gaol, in the neighbourhood of Hewit. But though she had the cypher of a husband, Ebenezer Beare, yet, as he bore no weight in the family, he was never mentioned; neither had he any more influence over her than a mouse over a cat; so that the residence always went by the name of Mrs. Beare's. She was remarkably expert at procuring gratifications for the men; an exit for those women who were troublesome wives; and abortion for those who were not.

With this singular couple, of opposite character, lived an harmless girl, Rosamond Ollorrenshaw, who, under such an accomplished tutoress, could not be long either ignorant or innocent.

Hewit and his wife frequented this house separately, while Mrs. Beare appeared the friend of both. He was pitied, as groaning under the burden of a hated wife; and she, as starving under a tyrannical husband. A criminal connexion was supposed, and perhaps with truth, to have taken place between him and both mistress and maid. The mistress being a wife, could have no future expectations of John; but the maid had; however it was determined between the parties, that Mrs. Hewit must quit the world. Her famished condition exciting the supposed tenderness of Mrs. Beare, she invited her to eat some pancakes; these were mixed by the mistress, but fried and served up by the maid; and in them was infused a quantity of arsenick, that in three hours operated in death. This happened on Saturday. The surgeons opened the body; suspicion fell where it ought; the town was in a tumult; and all the parties were committed to prison on Sunday night.

It is probable Hewit had an affection for Rosamond; for at their trial, when he
 P found

found he could not be saved himself, he endeavoured to save her: the Judge having asked her whether Mrs. Beare was privy to the poison, or ordered her to administer it; John trod upon her toe, that she might tell the truth and save herself; but she unfortunately mistook the hint for its reverse, and answered *no;* by which she saved the life of her mistress, and lost her own. While the two criminals, under sentence of death, attended divine service at St. Peter's, John rendered her every civility. Heavily ironed, and half-dead with the apprehension of her approaching fate, she could scarcely rise from her knees, when he took her round the waist in the face of a crowded church, and tenderly raised her. They walked to the place of execution, he in a suit of dark grey with black cuffs and trimmings; she in a drab gown, and hat which nearly covered her face. I think she leaned upon his arm. At the end of their dreadful journey, they both stripped, and appeared in their shrouds. She, unable to stand, rested upon the halter, after

being

being tied up, and expired before the cart moved. He was pitied; but she lamented.

Though Mrs. Beare was acquitted, the world was well convinced she was the wicked authoress of that mischief, by which three people had recently lost their lives: they were therefore solicitous to take her's. For this purpose, several indictments were preferred against her, at the next Assizes: one, for entering into a treaty with a young fellow to take away his wife, and furnish him with a better; but he had the prudence to communicate it to the unsuspecting victim, which defeated the scheme. Another, for receiving five guineas from a lady at Nottingham, to procure abortion. A third, for destroying the fœtus by the insertion of an instrument resembling an iron skewer. But though these were crimes of an atrocious nature, and sufficiently blackened by the counsel, yet, being unknown to the law, except by the vague name of *misdemeanors*, it had not provided an adequate punishment. This wholesale dealer in human destruction was only sentenced to

P 2 stand

stand two market-days in the pillory, and sustain three years imprisonment. I saw her, August 18, 1732, with an easy air ascend the hated machine, which overlooked an enraged multitude. All the apples, eggs, and turnips, that could be bought, begged, or stolen, were directed at her devoted head. The stagnate kennels were robbed of their contents, and became the cleanest part of the street. The pillory, being out of repair, was unable to hold a woman in her prime, whose powers were augmented by necessity: she released herself; and, jumping among the crowd, with the resolution and agility of an amazon, ran down the Morlege, being pelted all the way; new kennels produced new ammunition; and she appeared a moving heap of filth. With difficulty they remounted her; and I saw the exasperated brother of the unfortunate Rosamond pull her with violence into the pillory by the hair. An human being in distress excites commiseration, whatever is the cause. Her punishment exceeded death. By the time they had

had fixed her, the hour expired, and she was carried to prison, an object which none cared to touch.

The next Friday she appeared again not as a young woman, but an old one, ill, swelled, and decrepid; she seemed to have advanced thirty years in one week. The keeper suspecting some finesse from the bulk of her head, took off ten or twelve coverings, among which was a pewter plate, fitted to the head, as a guard against the future storm. He tossed it among the crowd, and left no covering but the hair. The pillory being made stronger, and herself being weaker, she was fixed for the hour; where she received the severe peltings of the mob; and they, her groans and her prayers.——She afterwards sustained the three years imprisonment, recovered her health, her spirits, and her beauty; and at her enlargement was preceded by a band of music.—She died in the meridian of life.

1735. The most elegant building in the whole country, the steeple of All Saints,

was

was perhaps within a few minutes of utter ruin. Some fractures in the leaden roof demanding the solder and plumbing-iron, the young and inattentive plumber, to save the labour of carrying his hot iron up stairs, made a fire at the top of the steeple, upon a hearth of loose bricks. These he carelessly left. Some days elapsed, when a smoak was observed issuing from the battlements: the ascent was dangerous, but necessary. The aspect was dreadful; the roof was melted, the sleepers burnt, and the main beam consumed to the very edge of the wall which supported it.—— thus a master-piece of elegance was snatched from the flames in the moment of destruction.

1737. *Thomas Topham.*

It is curious to observe Nature step out of her common road, and enter the wonderful. To march in her usual track excites no admiration; but when, wanton in her play, she forms an O'Brien of eight feet; a Borowlaski of three; an admirable Creichton with every accomplishment; or a John Crosland with none; it raises astonishment.

We

We learnt from private accounts, well attested, that Thomas Topham, a man who kept a public house at Islington, performed surprizing feats of strength; as breaking a broomstick, of the first magnitude, by striking it against his bare arm; lifting two hogsheads of water; heaving his horse over the turnpike-gate; carrying the beam of a house, as a soldier his firelock, &c. But however belief might stagger, she soon recovered herself when this second Sampson appeared at Derby, as a performer in public, at a shilling each. Upon application to Alderman Cooper, for leave to exhibit, the magistrate was surprized at the feats he proposed; and, as his *appearance* was like that of other men, he requested him to strip, that he might examine whether he was *made* like them; but he was found to be extremely muscular. What were hollows under the arms and hams of others, were filled up with ligaments in him.

He appeared near five feet ten, turned of thirty, well-made, but nothing singular;
he

he walked with a small limp; he had formerly laid a wager, the usual decider of disputes, that three horses could not draw him from a post, which he should clasp with his feet; but the driver giving them a sudden lash, turned them aside, and the unexpected jerk had broken his thigh.

The performances of this wonderful man, in whom were united the strength of twelve, were, rolling up a pewter-dish of seven pounds, as a man rolls up a sheet of paper—holding a pewter quart at arms length, and squeezing the sides together like an egg-shell—lifting two hundred weight with his little finger, and moving it gently over his head.—The bodies he touched seemed to have lost their powers of gravitation.—He also broke a rope, fastened to the floor, that would sustain twenty hundred weight—lifted an oak table six feet long with his teeth, though half a hundred weight was hung to the extremity: a piece of leather was fixed to one end for his teeth to hold, two of the feet stood upon his knees, and he

raised

raised the end with the weight higher than that in his mouth—he took Mr. Chambers, vicar of All Saints, who weighed 27 stone, and raised him with one hand—his head being laid on one chair, and his feet on another, four people, 14 stone each, sat upon his body, which he heaved at pleasure—he struck a round bar of iron, one inch diameter, against his naked arm, and at one stroke bent it like a bow. Weakness and feeling seemed fled together.

Being a master of music, he entertained the company with *Mad Tom*. I heard him sing a solo to the organ in St. Warburgh's church, then the only one in Derby; but though he might perform with judgement, yet the voice, more terrible than sweet, scarcely seemed human. Though of a pacific temper, and with the appearance of a gentleman, yet he was liable to the insults of the rude. The hostler at the Virgin's-inn, where he resided, having given him disgust, he took one of the kitchen-spits from the mantlepiece, and bent it round his neck like a hand-

handkerchief; but as he did not chuse to tuck the ends in the hostler's bosom, the cumbrous ornament excited the laugh of the company, till he condescended to untye his iron cravat. Had he not abounded with good-nature, the men might have been in fear for the safety of their persons, and the women for that of their pewter-shelves, as he could instantly roll up both. One blow with his fist would for ever have silenced those heroes of the bear-garden, Johnson and Mendoza.

1745. *The Rebellion.*

So called because it proved abortive: had it succeeded, it would have borne another name.

James, son of James the Second, only surviving heir of the unfortunate House of Stuart, and better known by the name of *The Pretender*, having attained the vigour of life, made two attempts, one in 1708, and the other in 1715, to regain the dominions of his ancestors; but, miscarrying in both, and age stealing on, he let his title sleep.—His son Charles, encouraged by by the powers of youth, a handsome person, an engaging address, a necessary share of ambition to stimulate to action, the promises of assistance from the European Courts, with whom England was at war, the engagements of the Highland chiefs, and, above all, the *faithful* assurances of the English to declare in his favour, landed in Scotland, August 10, 1745.

The small, but bold stroke at Preston-Pans, raised the credit of his arms. But as the mind which receives favours loses its consequence, so Charles, though possessed of mental powers, was never able to guide his own councils. His chiefs, who had ventured their all in his cause, thought they had a right to direct: this introduced confusion.

Assistance from foreign courts arrived slowly; the French forgot more than *half* their promises; and the English nearly *all;* yet the unhappy wanderer, with hasty strides, entered Derby on Wednesday, December the fourth, in his way to St James's. His artillery consisting of

thir-

thirteen pieces, was stationed upon Nunsgreen; his troops were dispersed through the town, and amounted to nearly the number of the inhabitants. Bells, bonfires, and proclamations, were, as usual, the first orders; horses, arms, and the delivery of public money, were the next.

Instead of marching forward the succeeding day, as was expected, a council of war was held privately at the headquarters, over which the Prince presided, but had not the leading voice. Many of the chiefs spoke. Their situation was critically examined. It was urged, " That they had followed their Prince with alacrity; that their love for his cause was equal to the hazard they run. That the French had not fulfilled their engagements in sending the necessary supplies, nor in making a diversion in the West to draw the military attention. That the English promises were still more delusive; for they had been given to understand, as soon as the Prince's standard should be erected in England, the majority would run
with

with eagerness to join it; instead of which they had raised only one slender regiment in their long march, which barely supplied their travelling losses. That the English were extremely loyal to the House of Stuart, when warmed by a good fire and good liquor; but the warmth of their fire, their liquor, and their loyalty, evaporated together. That they were then in the centre of an enemy's country, with a handful of men; to retreat was dangerous; but to proceed must be certain destruction." It was therefore determined to march back towards Scotland the next morning, and retrieve their affairs; which rendered Derby famous for the advance and retreat of that small and ill-appointed army, which shook a throne, and terrified a kingdom.—Thus the deluded Chevalier, before he left the Continent, had tried and determined his cause by hearing *one side* only; he forgot that another was to appear, by far the most numerous, which loudly declared for the Brunswick interest. —A retreat was the only wise step that
could

could be taken; for the Duke of Cumberland, son to George the Second, in the bloom of youth, and famous for intrepidity, was crossing the country from Lichfield to meet him, at the head of a superior army, and that of veterans, well supplied, in high spirits, and attached to their leader; so that about two days must have brought on a battle and inevitable ruin.

The behaviour of these desperate adventurers, while at Derby, is well described by Hugh Bateman, Esq. in St. Mary-gate, in a letter, written with more candour than was the practice of the times.——At eleven o'clock two of the van-guard entered, seized Mr. Stamford's house, went to the George-inn, and demanded billets for 9,000 men. They then enquired for the magistrates and their formalities, but were told they were fled; which answer satisfied. However, they afterwards seized upon Alderman Cooper, too lame to run away, and obliged him to proclaim the Prince.

In a short time 30 more, in the same uniform, which was blue, with scarlet waistcoats

waistcoats and gold-lace, arrived, commanded by Lord Balmerino. They were drawn up in the market-place, where they continued till three; when Lord Elcho arrived with 150, the remainder of the corps, being the Prince's life-guard. They were fine figures, well dressed; but their horses were jaded. Soon after the main body entered, six or eight a-breast; a mixture of every rank, from childhood to old age, from the dwarf to the giant, chiefly in deranged dresses, marked with dirt and fatigue. They carried eight standards, white, with red crosses. They were ushered in by the bag-pipes, that ancient Northern music, which raises the spirit of the martial Highlander. At dusk the Prince arrived on foot with his guards. He was tall, straight, slender, and handsome, dressed in a green bonnet laced with gold, a white bob-wig, the fashion of the day, a Highland plaid, and broad sword. He took up his quarters at the bottom of Full-street, in Lord Exeter's house; the Duke of Athol was at the house of Thomas Gisborn, Esq. Bridgegate;

gate; the Duke of Perth at Mrs. Rivett's, in the Morlege; Lord Elcho at Mr. Storer's; Lord George Murray at Mr. Heathcote's; Lord Pitslego at Mr. Meynell's; Old Gordon, of Glenbucket, at Alderman Smith's; Lord Nairn at Mr. John Bingham's; all in the market-place. Lady Ogilvie, Mrs. Murray, and others of distinction, lodged at Mr. Francis's in the Corn-market. The chief officers chose the best gentlemen's houses. Many of the inhabitants had forty or fifty of various ranks quartered upon them, and some a hundred.

Articles of dress were applied for, as being much wanted; some they had with money; but more without. A list of those people was procured who had associated and subscribed for the support of government; whom they obliged to pay the same sums to them. They demanded the land-tax, excise, &c. and actually received about £.2,500. They demanded also one hundred pounds from the Post-office, which was declined; they reduced it to fifty; but this not being complied with, they took away a post-chaise.

During

During their stay at Derby, *Cappoch,* whom the Chevalier had made bishop of Carlisle, preached at All Saints.—They beat up for volunteers, at five shillings advance, and five guineas when they arrived in London; but they were joined by three people only; *Cook,* a travelling journeyman blacksmith; *Edward Hewit,* a butcher, brother to John who was executed with Rosamond; and *James Sparks,* a stocking-maker; men of degraded life and sullied character. The eager *Sparks* could not wait their arrival, but met them in their approach to Derby, and accosted the leading officer in the most joyful terms, " This is the day," says he, " I have long wished for;" seized his piece, and hugged it to his bosom as a treasure. He also directed the gentlemen to suitable quarters; gave in the characters of the inhabitants; pointed out the friend and the foe; who was to be favoured, and who oppressed. He also guided the out-parties to the seats of the neighbouring gentry, among others, to that of Hugo Meynell, Esq. at Bradley; where, making

Q free

free with the liquors, he was left in the cellar completely intoxicated; the rebels themselves declaring, " he was not worth their regard." His protectors having fled towards the North, while he remained in the cellar, he was seized and carried before Thomas Gisborn, Esq. a spirited magistrate, who governed the men, was partial to the women, and excited a dread in all. He committed him to prison. Sparks was sent to York; where in November following, he was tried, condemned, and executed. Cook and Hewit escaped.

In their retreat from Derby, Friday the sixth, the Prince rode a black horse, said to have been Colonel Gardiner's, who was slain at Preston Pans.

When these unwelcome visitants had quitted the place, the magistrates ordered a return of their number in every house, during both the nights, which perhaps is the most correct muster-roll ever taken:

First night . . 7008.
Second night . . 7148.

If

If we allow for the royal guard, that of the artillery and baggage, the scouts in various parts of the neighbourhood, with the patroles, and the sentinels, of the principal officers, their number was probably about 8000.

Perhaps history cannot produce an instance of so small a number of men, so ill supplied, making a November march of so great an extent, in a remarkably wet winter, into the centre of a powerful enemy's country, and surrounded with continual dangers, who were able to retreat, and who did so little mischief. The Prince was of a mild temper, much averse to cruelty or depredation. Horses, arms, ammunition, and public money, in all similar cases, are deemed lawful plunder. They frequently paid their quarters; more frequently it was not expected. If they took people's shoes, it was because they had none of their own; and no voice speaks so loud as that of necessity: if they omitted payment, it was because they had no money.

1768.

1768. The King of Denmark arrived at the George Inn.

EMINENT MEN.

Distinguished characters demand the tribute of remembrance. To record the man who shines, is an inducement for others to emerge from darkness. To read the Hero, strikes fire into those particles of the composition which light up the Hero; thus the history of Alexander produced a Charles the Twelfth; Descartes was excelled by a Newton; and Boyle by a Priestley. Hidden excellencies lose half their value. To hold up the worthy, tends to make others worthy; as the Newgate Calendar tends to form the rascal. It is to the adequate pen of a Kippis we owe that vast group of characters which excite others to merit fame by emulation.

The eminent in Derby have been lost for want of the historian; but we can no more suppose, from their non-appearance, that they did not exist, than that a field did

not

not bear crops for centuries past, because nobody has informed us that it did.

Only two persons of exalted character are recorded, and that in Gough's edition of The Britannia.

Dr. Thomas Linacre,

whose family are yet residents, under the name of Linney, was bred at Oxford, where he pursued his studies with great attention, particularly that of physic. Quitting the university, he travelled for improvement, and spent a considerable part of his life at Florence and at Rome, where he practised with remarkable success. His learning was great and general. The Duke of Tuscany shewed him many favours, and pronounced him the politest scholar of the age. He was intimate with men of the first eminence for letters, as Dean John Colet, the great Erasmus, &c. which proves him to have been a Theologist.

After studying in Italy, he returned to London, and fixed his abode in Knight-
Rider-

Rider-Street. He became the first physician to Henry the Seventh, the Eighth, Edward the Sixth, and the Princess Mary; also physician and tutor to Prince Arthur. Able talents, cultivated by attention, under the smiling beams of Royalty, could not fail of a plentiful harvest of wealth. He founded two public lectures at Oxford for the study of physic; and one at Cambridge. This ornament of human nature, out of mere love to his species, rescued the Medical Art from the bold empiric and the illiterate monk, by instituting the College of Physicians in London. He erected the building upon the site of his own residence; afterwards burnt down by the great fire. Nor did he forget the place of his nativity; for he left an annual benefaction to Derby, yet called *Linacre's Charity*. His powers may be said to have been employed in the service of man in a double capacity; for having practised with success the art of healing the body, and his mind being tinctured with a religious cast, he became, towards the close of life, a priest, and attempted

tempted to heal the soul; in which profession he died in 1524, and was interred under a stately monument in St. Paul's Cathedral.

John Flamstead.

Whether a man shall acquire a fortune of ten pounds, or of ten thousand, depends often upon a trifling circumstance; an incident that at the time it happens, appears of no moment. A person, I well knew, had excellent talents for the Bar; his uncle was a shoe-maker, and wished *him* a shoe-maker; the balance was exactly even; a trifle turned the scale, and he starved upon the *last* for life.—Thomas Jordan had the offer of a valuable farm, which carried with it a fortune; at the same time a corn-mill presented itself, supplied by one weak spring: timorous, he hesitated a moment; took the mill, and never amassed a groat. —William L—— had an intimate friend, who enlisted for a private soldier in the war of forty-one. He strongly solicited L—— to enlist with him. L—— more than

than half consented; but, waving the decision till morning, turned his thoughts to business, and acquired a fortune of £.20,000.

There is also but a slender barrier between the honest man and the knave; between the excellent philosopher and the halter.

John Flamstead, the great mathematician, who, in 1675, was concerned in erecting the Observatory at Greenwich, and in the reigns of Queen Anne and George the First presided over it as Astronomer-royal, was a native of Derby, some say Denby; his father, however, resided in Derby. John was born in 1646, and continued in Derby till 1670. The first rudiments of his extensive learning he acquired at the free-school in St. Peter's church-yard. Among the early follies of youth, he was accused, with some degenerate companions, as being concerned in a highway robbery, for which he was tried and condemned. Circumstances and friends appearing in his favour, the royal pardon was procured

from

from Charles the Second. This piece of discredit was not generally known in after-life. The bent of his own mind being then pursued, he became one of the greatest ornaments of man. He discovered new worlds in the heavens, which he communicated to posterity. Instead of pursuing unjustly the things of this world, he followed with applause those of others; and may be said to have set his affections on things above. He died in 1719, at the age of 73, leaving a most amiable character. Among his papers the pardon was found. John Webb, who was an intimate acquaintance of his, and afterwards of mine, gave me the anecdote.

Thomas Parker Earl of Macclesfield, if not a native, claims a place, as having been long a resident, and finding in Derby the road to riches, honours, fame, and a title. He was born in 1667; was a private attorney, and resided many years in Bridge-gate, at the foot of the bridge, in the house next to the Three Crowns. Abilities and industry procured him practice;

practice brought money; and money consequence. These united initiated him into the office of Recorder; which opened a wider field for his talents. The man who has a capacity for great things, and is assisted by activity, never stops at small; success accelerates his actions. Mr. Parker soon became a pleader at the bar; travelled the Midland circuit; acquired additional esteem, business, and property; was denominated the Silver-tongued Counsel; and found interest enough, in 1705, to cause himself to be returned a member for the borough, with Lord James Cavendish, son to the first Duke of Devonshire. He was chosen again in 1707.

Having now got into the political world, where his talents beamed in full brightness, without the danger of an eclipse, he made rapid strides towards preferment. Here we find him *Sir* Thomas. The Commons, sensible of his powers, chose him one of their managers in the famous trial of Dr. Sacheverell in 1709, which he conducted with great ability. Of all the speeches, his

his are the most nervous. If the Doctor got imaginary honours by this trial, Sir Thomas acquired real; for before the election in 1710, he was made Lord Chief Justice of the King's Bench. He then quitted Derby. Being offered the Chancellor's seals, he refused them, because his sentiments did not coincide with those of the Harleian ministry. George the First, entertaining the highest opinion of his merit, created him Baron Parker in 1716; Viscount Parker of Ewelme in 1718. And now he accepted the seals with safety.

He was created Earl of Macclesfield in 1721; and continued Lord Chancellor six years; when he was accused, and brought to trial, for selling places in Chancery; and fined £.30,000, which I believe he paid. He lost the Chancellorship of course. The King called for the council-book, and with a sigh, some said with a tear, dashed out his name.

There is not a character more hunted than a disgraced favourite; his excellencies are forgotten; and his errors magnified:
" Stafford-

"Staffordshire, it was said, had produced three of the greatest rogues that ever existed, Jack Shepard, Jonathan Wild, and Lord Macclesfield." The man who rises to elevation, draws the envy as well as the eyes of the beholder. If I cannot ascend to his eminence, I have a right to bring him down to mine. The Lord Chancellor had certainly committed a fault; but such a one as is every day committed. Are not votes, places, and interest, continual articles of traffic? Are not half the people in office shuffled into their places by sale? Have not votes of all kinds been long put up for hire; some of them, being of small value, will scarcely bear a dinner and a gallon of ale; while others of a more exalted nature amply furnish a table round the year? Does not one man oblige another with his interest for a return, which is only another word for purchase? Even church-livings frequently find a price. Lord Macclesfield's was a species of bribery of a milder nature than is generally practised. If he disposed of a clerkship to a person fit for

the

the office, which, from his able judgement, we may reasonably conclude, his country could no way be affected, whether he sold it, or gave it: but if a minister, or his underling, buys a vote, his country may suffer. If Lord Macclesfield's clerk does his duty, all concerned are benefited; but if a patron chance to be an improper judge, and sell a benefice, the whole parish is injured. Unhappily for the Chancellor, party rage ran high; and his enemies fixed a brand upon his name, of that magnitude which never wore out. This happened to the worthy Lord Verulam, who, for a trifling set of buttons, raised the clamour of a kingdom, as if that kingdom were honester than himself. Discovery constituted the fault. If you or I, my dear Reader, never sold a place, perhaps it was because we had none to sell; hence our fair character arises from necessity.

The accomplished Lord Macclesfield, in the height of prosperity, did not forget the place where the scene of his elevation opened; for in 1722, twelve years after,

he

he contributed one hundred guineas, and his son, Lord Parker, twenty, towards the erection of All Saints. He retired, during the last eight years of his life, the philosopher and the friend; when, seized with a strangury, he resigned his existence, as a Christian, on the 28th of April, 1732, at the age of 65.

Benjamin Parker

resided in Bridge-gate; was a writer of books, a maker of stockings, and consequently a poor man. He who sells the labour of others, may become rich; but not the stockinger, who sells none but his own. He wrote Philosophical *Meditations*, and dedicated it to the Duke of Devonshire, who took some notice of him. Encouraged by this mark of favour, he wrote a second part, and dedicated it to Queen Caroline, who took none. The pride of an Author taught him to aspire; disappointment, to fall.—He dipped his pen into that violent Trinitarian controversy which happened about the year 1735, which put the nation

into

into a flame, and was the last grand effort to maintain a falling doctrine. He also wrote a treatise upon the Longitude. His style was more elevated than himself; his reasonings were fair and candid; his penetration deep.

John Whitehurst.

It will be granted, if a man spends forty years of the prime of his life in Derby, he may be called *A Derby Man;* John Whitehurst, therefore, is the legal subject of my pen. This great philosopher, mechanic, and worthy man, was born at Congleton in 1713, where his ancestors are said to have resided, upon a small estate, more than 700 years. He was one of those few whom Nature designed for *thinking* upon such abstruse subjects as cannot easily be *seen.* His researches penetrated the internal parts of the earth, that he might develope the contents, and appropriate them to the use of man. The Peak, in the neighbourhood of his residence, furnished an ample field for his philosophic mind. His taste for mechanics sent him into Ireland, to inspect a curious clock. He was bred a watch-maker, and opened a shop in 1735 at Derby; but, that being a corporate town, he found himself embarrassed because he was not a burgess. He therefore, in 1737, made a clock for the Guildhall, as the purchase of his freedom; which, in telling truth, still praises its maker. He afterwards fabricated the chimes for All Saints; and constructed the clock for the steeple, which teaches another to keep that time its maker has lost for ever.

He wrote, "An Enquiry into the Original State and Formation of the Earth," in quarto; wherein he treads upon new ground, and advances positions unknown to former philosophy; the work of years, reflection, and minute research. He was admitted a member of the Royal Society; and laid before that learned body some curious papers. He was also a member of several other Philosophical Societies of respectable men.

Being

Being appointed stamper of the weights in 1775, for regulating the gold coin, he left Derby, and his occupation, to reside in London. He also wrote Thermometrical Observations; an Account of a Machine for raising Water; Experiments upon Ignited Substances; an Attempt towards obtaining invariable Measures of Length, Capacity, and Weight, from the Mensuration of Time; a Treatise on Ventilation, particularly on Smoaky Chimnies; an evil under which half the world groans, and which every petty builder can cure, but still the evil remains: if it should ever be removed, it must be by a Whitehurst. He also examined the nature of garden-stoves, the properties of air, the laws of fluids, &c. which, I think, have not been published.

He was near six feet high, straight, thin, and wore his own dark-grey bushy hair; was plain in his dress; and had much the appearance of a respectable farmer. I saw him at Buxton in 1785, and wished his acquaintance; but though we sat at the same table, I could find no opportunity of introducing myself.

A change of habits is ill suited to advanced life. The man who has cherished his apron fifty years, parts with it as with an old friend. Little action, a more elegant style of living, and, above all, the infirmities of age, brought on complaints, which a long and lean form of body were unable to support: these terminated, as he foresaw, in a dissolution, which happened February 18, 1788, at the age of 75, in Bolt-Court, London, in the very house where, a few years before, died that great and self-taught philosopher, James Ferguson: in the same court also where died that great master of letters, Dr. Johnson.

There is a singular pleasure in writing the lives of great and worthy men. The writer is paid for his labour. It is also pleasing to the reader, and beneficial to the world. Part of this information is extracted from an account of this great man in the Universal Magazine, November 1788, drawn by an able pen.

" *Joseph*

"*Joseph Wright*,
" commonly called *Wright of Derby*,
" A very distinguished painter, was born at Derby, September 3, 1734. His father was an attorney there. In early life, he gave indications of a taste for mechanics, and those habits of attentive observation, which generally lead to perfection in the fine arts. In 1751, he came to London, and was placed with Hudson, the most eminent portrait-painter of the day, and who, lord Orford tells us, pleased the country gentlemen with " his honest similitudes, fair tied wigs, blue velvet coats, and white satin waistcoats, which he bestowed liberally on his customers." Wright used to lament that he could not receive much instruction from this master, but it is certain he at this time painted both portraits and historical pieces in a very capital style, of which his " Blacksmith's forge," " Air-pump, &c." are proofs. In 1773, after marrying, he visited Italy, and made great advances in his pro- fession.

fession. In 1775 he returned to England, and settled for two years at Bath, after which his residence was entirely at Derby.

" His attention was directed some years to portrait-painting; and from the specimens he has left, there can be no doubt that he would have stood in the first rank in this branch of the art, had he chosen to pursue it: but his genius was not to be circumscribed within such narrow limits, and therefore, at a mature age, he visited Italy, to study the precious remains of art which that country possessed. His fine drawings, after Michael Angelo (which have scarcely been seen except by his particular friends), and the enthusiasm with which he always spoke of the sublime original, evinced the estimation in which he held them; and from their extreme accuracy, they may be considered as faithful delineations of the treasures of the Capella Sestina. In 1782 he was elected an associate of the Royal Academy; but offended at Mr. Garvey's being chosen royal academician before himself, he resigned his associate's diploma

ploma in disgust, yet continued to exhibit at intervals with that society. In 1785 he made an exhibition of his own pictures at the auction room now Robins's, in the Great Piazza, Covent Garden. The collection consisted of twenty-four pictures.

" During his abode in Italy he had an opportunity of seeing a very memorable eruption of Vesuvius, which rekindled his inclination for painting extraordinary effects of light; and his different pictures of this sublime event stood decidedly *chef d'œuvres* in that line of painting; for who but Wright ever succeeded in fire or moonlights? His later pictures were chiefly landscapes, in which we are at a loss, whether most to admire the elegance of his outline, his judicious management of light and shade, or the truth and delicacy of his colouring; but of those, the greatest part have never been exhibited, as they were always purchased from the easel by amateurs who knew how to appreciate their value: a large landscape (his last work) now at Derby, being a view of the head of Ullswater, may be considered

amongst

amongst the finest of his works, and deservedly ranks with the most valued productions of Wilson, or even Claude himself.

"In the historical line, the Dead Soldier, which is now known by Heath's admirable print, would alone establish his fame, if his Edwin (in the possession of J. Milnes, esq. of Wakefield, who has also his Destruction of the Floating Batteries off Gibraltar, and some of his best landscapes), the two pictures of Hero and Leander, Lady in Comus, Indian Widow, and other historical subjects, had not already ascertained his excellence. His attachment to his native town, added to his natural modesty, and his severe application both to the theory and practise of painting, prevented his mixing with promiscuous society, or establishing his reputation by arts which he would never descend to practice. His friends long urged him to reside in London; but his family attachments, and love of retirement and study, were invincible, and he fell a victim to his unwearied attention to his profession. He died of a decline, Aug. 29, 1797. "His

"His pictures have been so much in request, that there is scarcely an instance of their ever having come into the hands of dealers; neither have his best works ever been seen in London: a strong proof of their intrinsic worth, and that no artifices were necessary to insure their sale. It is with pleasure, therefore, that we record, that his pecuniary circumstances were always affluent, and shew that the world has not been unmindful of his extraordinary talents, and also that, as a man, he enjoyed the friendship and esteem of all who had the pleasure of his acquaintance *."

Robert Bage.

If we find a pleasure in drawing a valuable character which has *left* the stage, that pleasure must be double when we treat of those who still adorn it; because we then revere both the *character* and the *man*. This, in the present case, is my pleasing task. The man I now delineate is a native of Derby, but left it at an early period.

* Chalmers's Biographical Dictionary, vol. XXXII.

He amuses the world and himself with novel productions, of a superior class, as Mount Henith, Barham Downs, The Fair Syrian, James Wallace, &c. wherein is an excellent picture of life, a full display of character, and sentiment. These have travelled to the Continent, passed through the Frankfort press, and appeared to the world in a German habit.

Although Fortune never made him conspicuous in the great world, she gave him what is preferable, affluence and content. In directing a paper-mill, may be found that head which is able to direct empires; that judgment, which can decide in difficult cases; a penetration which can fathom the human heart, and comprehend various systems of knowledge; a genius, which constitutes the companion for Newton in Philosophy; for Handel in Music; for Euclid in Mathematicks; a master of the living and dead languages; and all, like the wealth of a merchant who rises from nothing, acquired by himself. Nay, I should even rank him with that learned
body

body the Physicians, if he were not defective in one branch of the profession—the art of killing. That rectitude, which is rarely found, is here obscured from the public eye; but is a pearl of great price, and a credit to our species. Though a diminutive figure, yet one of the most amiable of men; and though in some points a Sceptic, yet one of the best. I have known him 56 years; his friendship is an honour I have long possessed; to which I shall add another, by uniting his name with my own. Should he frown at this liberty, I will say twice as much; should he retort, I will take my revenge by drawing a complete character; for he has amply furnished me with materials.

He died Sept. 1, 1801, after our intimacy had continued sixty-six years.

GENTLEMEN'S SEATS NEAR DERBY.

I have wandered with the reader into every street and corner of what has often been pronounced, "A pretty town, though not a large one;" and what is now a thriving one. We have examined its antiquity, with not only its ancient and modern structures; but called into existence those that are gone. We have seen its charities, police, and honours; the nature of its government, and its religious conduct; which last did not shine in the most amiable light. We have followed the arts in their rise and progress; the amusements of the inhabitants; the occurrences of the times; and the productions of Genius. We shall now take a wider circle, though small: and enumerate the families, and their seats, which surround it. Having surveyed the planet, we shall attempt its ring.

The neighbouring villages of Derby produce more gentlemen than is usually found

in

in so small a compass; and some of them boast a long antiquity. Many of their names are familiar in history for talents, hospitality, patriotism, honours, and arms.

Pole of Radburn.

This family are proprietors of a handsome seat at Radburn (Redbrook), five miles West of Derby, where they have resided in affluence about four hundred years; but their predecessors, by the female line, have enjoyed it some centuries longer.

Little Over,

one mile distant, was the residence of a branch of the ancient family of Harpur, now of Heathcoat of Derby, by a marriage with the heiress. Nothing can be said in favour of the house, except its antiquity; but every thing may in favour of its situation, which is charming beyond conception.

Every of Eggington.

Upon the fertile banks of the Dove, near its junction with the Trent, and eight miles

miles from Derby, stands the elegant seat of the family of Every; upon the head of which Charles the First, in 1641, conferred the title of Baronet. In 1655 the Commonwealth confiscated the estates of more than three thousand of the Nobility and Gentry, who had favoured the Royal Cause. Sir Simon Every was one. The proprietors, who were not recusants, were allowed to compound for a stipulated sum. The lowest price of redemption, in this cruel catalogue, was ten shillings; and the highest, Sir Amias Meredith's, twenty thousand pounds. The whole amount of the composition was one million, three hundred and five thousand, two hundred and ninety-nine pounds, four shillings, and seven-pence. Sir Henry Every paid for his father, Sir Simon, one hundred and ten pounds.

Burdet of Formark.

Formark stands upon the beautiful banks of the Trent. It was the residence, till the reign of Queen Elizabeth, of the family

mily of *Francis;* when that of Burdet succeeded by marriage. This family ascends into great antiquity; the founder makes part of that list of archers who came over with William. The title of Baronet entered the family in 1618. The present Baronet erected this noble mansion in 1755; and has been favoured with an uncommon share of temporal benefits, by enjoying the honour and estate more than seventy-four years, double the portion assigned to man: Fortune even waited for him at his birth; nor can it be said that he has yet quitted the precincts of youth. Immortality cannot be allowed on this side the grave*; all that *can*, are health and content, till time wears out the system. Whoever holds these, enjoys the principal riches of the universe: all beyond is food for vanity.

* Sir Robert Burdet, LL. D. the fourth Baronet, died Feb. 22, 1797, in his 81st year. He was the posthumous son of his father, who died eleven days only before his own father Sir Robert Burdet, the third Baronet. Sir Francis Burdet succeeded his grandfather in 1797. EDIT.

Harpur

Harpur of Calke.

Calke is a small village eight miles South of Derby, the residence of the ancient family of Harpur, whose pedigree may be traced more than six hundred years; at which time they were inhabitants of Chesterton in Warwickshire. About four hundred years ago, they were of Rushall in Staffordshire; and about two centuries back of Swarkstone, when they were very numerous. As the sun emerging from obscurity, they quickly covered the adjacent villages. One branch, as above, was planted at Little-Over; another at Breadsall; a third at Calke; and a fourth at Twyford; all in the vicinity of Derby.—In process of time, the *members* of this fertile family dwindled; but not the riches, which chiefly centered in one focus, that of Calke. The head of the family was the first Baronet, created by Charles the First, Sept. 8, 1626. They have often supplied the county with representatives and sheriffs.—Sir John Harpur's estate was charged with a fine of five hundred and seventy-eight pounds, eighteen shillings

shillings and two-pence, because he was found in the interest of Charles the First; and his relation, John Harpur, of Swarkston, with one of four thousand pounds,

Melburn (Mill-Brook),
seven miles South, the seat of Lord Viscount Melbourne.—This village is populous, and famous for Religion, which appears in a variety of forms; but more famous for an ancient castle, though ill adapted *for* one; in which John Duke of Bourbon, of the blood-royal of France, taken at Agincourt, was confined a prisoner nineteen years. This castle fell in the quarrel between the Roses; is wholly destroyed except one wall, two yards thick, ten high, and twice as long. Lord Melbourne's house, though worth the notice of the stranger, is not *much* noticed by its master. The place abounds with wood and water; but the prospects are defective.

Borrow, of Castle Field.
Joining the town on the East, is the neat residence of Thomas Borrow, Esq.; erected

erected by his great-grand father in the reign of George the First. Great care has been taken to secure it from the eye of the traveller. The premises abound with well-disposed clumps, nearly perfect. No situation can be ill, which has Derby on one side, the fine river Derwent on another, the spacious London road on a third, and a beautiful park on the fourth.

Shuttleworth of Aston.

Aston is a village six miles from Derby. It stands on a charming peninsula, formed by the Trent and the Derwent, which consists of meadows, fields, hills, woods, and water, and is one continued scene of pleasure-ground. In the centre of these beauties is the seat of the family of Shuttleworth, more properly, of Holden. Here is also a small neat house of the late Joseph Greaves, Esq.; who served the office of Sheriff in 1765; now of Charles Best, Esq.

Shardlow,

Shardlow,

six miles East; the seat of Leonard Fosbroke, Esq. who a few years ago added two wings to his house, which have an admirable effect. I considered this the most beautiful situation that a flat country could allow, till that vile taste was adopted of choaking the aspect with trees. Woods are the first ornament of a villa when planted with judgement; but the reverse if attempted without.

Stanhope of Elvaston.

Four miles from Derby, in the same direction, is Elvaston, which, for two hundred years, was the residence of this family, a family well respected, and from which the town often chose its representatives. The head of this house being an intimate friend of George the First, he conferred upon him a peerage; and George the Second, in 1742, created him Earl of Harrington.—The building is not modern; neither has it much claim to elegance;

gance; the situation has less; and it is rendered still more disgusting, by being smothered with trees. When an architect makes choice of a bad spot, by the side of a good one, the eye is doubly hurt.

Wilmot, of Chaddesdon and of Osmaston.

These are two villages, each a mile from Derby, and two from each other, possessed by two gentlemen of the name of *Wilmot*, both Baronets. The elder branch is that of Chaddesdon. The house is elegant, the situation more so, and the descendants of the family have there succeeded each other about 250 years.

A younger son of this house, in the reign of Charles the Second, by following the law, picked up such plentiful gleanings as enabled him to place himself, and an opulent succession, at Osmaston. To change the figure, he climbed with *safety* that slippery ladder, the law, by which a few rise to eminence, but many fall.— This house, viewed from the London-road, is one of the most beautiful pieces of architecture I ever beheld. Let the eye of the Critic detach any of the parts, and he will find it complete; let him view the whole, and it is still perfect. The style and symmetry are admirable, and delight the beholder; but the place in which it stands is inadequate to so pleasing a structure. The timber, which is ill disposed, might, at a small expence, form a striking beauty.

Risley,

eight miles East, was the residence of one of the most antient families in the county, of the name of Willoughby, which also held a place among the first of its gentry. The fine old fabric stood in as bad a place as art could direct. But now, alas! the family, the noble estate, and the venerable hall, are mouldered to destruction. That spot, which afforded the most generous hospitality to man, now affords grass for the horse.

Hopwell,

Hopwell,

two miles nearer Derby; a delightful situation, which commands an admirable prospect, though abounding with woods; late the habitation of the family of Key, one of whom was sheriff in 1678; afterwards of Lake; now of Thomas Pares, Esq. F. S. A.

Locko (Lockhay),

four miles off, but in the same direction; a handsome house, pleasantly situated, and well adapted for retirement; the seat of the Gilberts; then the Coopers; and now the Lowes; all of one family. Henry Gilbert was charged with a fine of six hundred and eighty pounds by Oliver's Parliament. Here sweetly tuned his lyre that celebrated poet Gilbert Cooper, who wrote the little poem to his wife, which perhaps has done what few poems have, pleased every reader:

"Away, let nought to Love displeasing," &c.

Holden

Holden of Derley.

One mile above Derby, in a beautiful vale upon the rich banks of the Derwent, where the monk prayed and feasted, till Henry and destruction overtook him, is the noble mansion of Derley-hall, possessed by Robert Holden, Esq.; the head of an ancient family. The premises were the property of *Heath*, and prior to that, of *Woolley*.

Curzon of Kedleston.

The founder of this family was an attendant upon the prosperous sword of William, when he reduced this unhappy country under the Norman yoke. He appears to have been an officer of rank, by being rewarded with estates in three counties, Oxford, Berks, and Devon; perhaps in four, that of Derby; for his son, nay, I believe himself, was possessed of Kedleston: so that the family has held the manor about 700 years. Perhaps a parallel instance cannot be produced in the neighbourhood

bourhood of Derby, except in the family of *Gresley*, who have been proprietors of Drakelow during the same period. The land, a stranger to purchase, seems to rejoice, as never changing its master; and the Lord, as enjoying a permanent title, without one deed to support it. What is farther remarkable, both families retain their Norman names. The Curzons have occasionally held the offices of sheriff and representative ever since those offices were instituted. They were Knights when the Crown wanted money, and Esquires when it did not, till 1641, when Sir John Curzon, perhaps for a thousand pounds, brought the title of Baronet into the family; and George the Third, in 1761, advanced the present possessor to the dignity of Lord Scarsdale.

The Curzons were famous for riches; and the place of their abode for hospitality.

The house, the work of the present owner, and of thirty years, is one of the most superb in the kingdom. It is made whatever money or genius could make it.

All

All the beauties that art can assemble are united in the building, the furniture, and the park! a terrestrial paradise, too delightful for a man to wish to quit, that he might follow his fore-fathers. — I shall wave a particular description of this noble edifice, because *Pilkington*, in his " Present State of Derbyshire," has given one, to which I refer the Reader.

Perhaps two hundred thousand pounds lie under this spacious roof, consequently Lord Scarsdale sits at the rent of ten thousand a year! a rent that would perform wonders. To receive it, would make a man forget *himself;* to *pay* it, would make even a hero tremble. Could it be saddled upon a man in the commercial line, he would dream that his name had entered the Gazette. Surprized into such a rent, even the Grand Sovereign of the Queen of Isles would start, recoil, and speak quick. A rent equal to that of a considerable town: equal perhaps to two thirds of Derby; for I estimate the whole amount of the houses at about fifteen thousand a year.—One

year's

year's income, distributed among the random poor, would make them more idle, and prove destructive to the manufactures; if among economic tradesmen, it would like a guide-post direct them the road to affluence; if to one hundred of the fair sex, it would buy as many husbands, and soon create a village; if to the like number of lovers, it would tend to separate the hearts that were uniting, and ruin the fair; delivered to an imprudent youth, he would destroy his health by wasting it; or to a miser, he would break his rest by keeping it; but in no case bring content, or ward off the effects of age.

Mundy of Markeaton.

An old hall, of wood and plaister, was taken down, and the present erected by the possessor about forty years ago. It is a beautiful structure, and stands in as beautiful a valley, with Derby in front, one mile distant.

The commerce of London, by which many families acquire fortunes, but few keep them was the rise of this. A successful ancestor, John Mundy, was lord-mayor in 1522. The smile of affluence exciting a desire to seat his descendants upon a permanency, he purchased the lordships of Markeaton, Mackworth, and Allestry, all upon the borders of Derby; to which were added, the manors of Shipley, Quarndon, and Osbiston. The family afterwards dividing into two branches, caused a division of the manors. Perhaps they were connected with this neighbourhood prior to that period, for Robert Mundy represented Derby in 1446.

Mackworth,

two miles West of Derby. This place was probably five hundred years ago the property of the ancient family of Touchet Lord Audley, who, being a man of the sword, and of great wealth, retained several Esquires in his service. To a favourite follower, who had distinguished himself under his banner at Poitiers in 1356, he gave the manor of Mackworth. This gentleman built

built a castle for his residence, and assumed the name of the village. His successors continued there some ages. But in the civil wars of Charles the First, that melancholy contest, which was to determine whether a man's person and property ought to be directed by himself or his Sovereign, this castle was destroyed. It is now in ruins.

Meynell of Langley.

Some houses, like that of Calke Hall, deserve a better situation; and some situations, like that of Langley, deserve a better house.

This place, which is four miles west of Derby, was the ancient residence of a more ancient family, commanders of an ample fortune; now in the name of Cheney, a descendant by the female line from the Meynells.—Incidents, seemingly beneath notice, not only characterize persons, but exhibit the different style of life between the last century and the present.—While the Meynell family were spending their

sober

sober evening by the glow of their own fire, a coach and six was heard rolling up to the door:—" Bring candles," says the lady of the mansion, with some emotion, while she stept forward to receive the guests; but instantly returning, " Light up a rush," said she; " it is only my cousin Curzon."

FINIS.

Printed by Nichols, Son, and Bentley,
Red Lion Passage, Fleet Street, London.

Books by the same Author,

Sold by NICHOLS, SON, *and* BENTLEY,

And BALDWIN, CRADOCK, *and* JOY.

1. BATTLE OF BOSWORTH FIELD, 1485. With LIFE OF RICHARD THE THIRD, till he assumed the Regal Power. By W. HUTTON, F. A. S. S. The Second Edition, with Additions by J. NICHOLS, F. S. A.; and Eleven Plates. Price 12s. boards. The Additions may be had separate, price 5s.

"Mr. Hutton's Battle of Bosworth Field contains a variety of circumstances relating to that important and decisive event, which have been unknown to our other Historians and Antiquaries. The Work is interesting and amusing, and may contribute to the Illustration of this dark period of History." *New Annual Review.*

"Bosworth Field appears to be classic ground with Mr. Hutton; and we speak not without sufficient authority when we affirm, that he has surveyed the favoured object of his researches with an attention, an ardour, and a perseverance, never before displayed by any English Historian or Antiquary." *Critical Review.*

2. HISTORY OF THE ROMAN WALL, describing its ancient state and present appearance. By W. HUTTON, F. A. S. S. The Second Edition, with Portrait, and many Plates, price 12s. bds.

"This Author's Tour to the Roman Wall has afforded us not less pleasure than information. That Reader must be saturnine indeed, who can peruse this Book without being amused." *Monthly Review, March* 1806.

"This is a very amusing and interesting portion of Topographical History. The lively and cheerful manners of the Author captivate the fancy; and we follow him through the progress of his journey with sympathy and curiosity." *New Annual Review.*

3. TRIP TO COATHAM, a Watering-place in the North Extremity of Yorkshire, with Plates, 10s. 6d.

4. HISTORY OF BIRMINGHAM, 3d edition, with Plates, 10s. 6d.

5. REMARKS ON NORTH WALES, with Plates, 7s. 6d.

6. COURTS OF REQUESTS, particularly that of Birmingham, described, 8s.

7. THE SCARBOROUGH TOUR in 1803; including a particular description of the City of York.

"This Work manifests traits of good sense, strokes of good humour, evidences of a tolerant spirit, and proofs of a decidedly virtuous turn of mind, which secure to the writer the esteem of every good reader." *Monthly Review, March* 1806.

"Mr. Hutton shews an intimate knowledge of his own country, and its annals. In this work he gives an entertaining description of York and its antiquities." *British Critic,* 1804.

8. LIFE OF WILLIAM HUTTON, written by himself, and published by his Daughter. 12s.

www.ingramcontent.com/pod-product-compliance
Ingram Content Group UK Ltd.
Pitfield, Milton Keynes, MK11 3LW, UK
UKHW030834290425
5676UKWH00045B/996